Scriabin: His Life and Times

Scriabin

Ye. Rudakova and A.I. Kandinsky
Translated by Tatyana Chistyakova

PAGANINIANA PUBLICATIONS, INC.
211 W. Sylvania Avenue, Neptune City, N. J. 07753

Contents

Preface: Portrait of the Composer as an Artist 9

Notes to Preface 39

1872-1891: Early Years; Moscow Conservatory;
    Beginnings as a Composer 43

1892-1902: After Graduation; First Artistic Period 59

1903-1908: Artistic Prime 77

1909-1915: The Final Years of Life and Work;
    Concert Career 99

Scriabin in Soviet Musical Life 119

Notes To Text 137

Index 141

Artists' conceptions of Scriabin at different stages of his career.

A 1909 picture of Scriabin, with autographed passages from Sonata no. 4 and *The Poem of Ecstasy*.

Preface

Portrait of the Composer as an Artist

Towards the end of the 1890s, on the threshold of the new century, Scriabin stood out among the young generation of Russian musicians for his exceptional and bright talent. This was revealed even in his comparatively early works containing that peculiar quality of "recognition" which is always a distinctive feature of the artist of genius, of the special harmony of his poetic images, and of the peculiarities of his musical language. Scriabin riveted the attention of his contemporaries by the many facets of his intellectual and artistic interests, by his "synthetic" self-expression: he was an innovative composer who extended the boundaries of music; he was at the same time a poet and a philosopher who in his music proclaimed the ideals of goodwill and light, and of the brotherhood of all people.

The particular traits of Scriabin's creative personality are closely linked to the era from which he came. Scriabin's work can be seen as the embodiment of the "élan" and the emotional impulses of the explosive revolutionary period of Russian life at the beginning of the 20th century. But his art is of our time as well. For over half a century, Scriabin's music has retained its power and still wins the hearts of people of different social worlds. Today, the composer's works also enchant listeners by the tremendous spiritual energy, the volcanic emotion, and the sense of heroic optimism they contain.

Both his individual gifts and the contemporary atmosphere — the intellectual and aesthetic interests of the people close to him — were of great importance in the molding of Scriabin's creative personality. Toward the end of the 1890s, the musical environment of Moscow was the medium for the composer's artistic formation. That was where the great traditions of "classical" Russian 19th century art were preserved. There was much that contributed to the impetuous development of his talent. First, studies with one of Moscow's leading piano teachers, Zverev, and contacts with fellow students like Rachmaninoff, Keneman, Maksimov, Levin. Later, at the Moscow Conservatory, he studied counterpoint with Sergei Taneyev and piano with Vassily Safonov. Safonov admired his pupil's keyboard talent, helped Scriabin in the post-conservatory years, and conducted his symphonies. Conservatory professors (Arensky being the only exception), fellow-students, and families of friends — all whole-hearted-

Scriabin's Nocturne in A flat major (1884), published in the *Music* magazine.

**Sergei Rachmaninoff (1873-1943), the great composer and pianist, a
fellow student of Scriabin's at the Conservatory.**

Fedor F. Keneman (1873-1937), pianist, conductor, and composer.

Frédéric Chopin (1810-1849), the favorite composer of the young
Scriabin. Painting by Delacroix.

Richard Wagner.

ly welcomed the young musician both as composer and pianist. His works were performed publicly even at the start of his career as a composer, and from the second half of the 1890s were a regular feature of Moscow and St. Petersburg concert programs. It was at that time that Scriabin became close to the famous St. Petersburg composers Glazunov and Liadov, as well as to music publisher Belaieff, who later became a solicitous friend and the publisher of Scriabin's works. The composer's initial public concert appearances, both at home and abroad, were a succession of triumphs. Between 1898 and 1903, Scriabin was a professor at the Moscow Conservatory (piano class).

At that time a special side of Scriabin's character, which one of his first biographers, Yu. D. Engel, later described, began to manifest itself: ". . . a clear sense of his exceptional gift, a sense which became more and more intense and acute as time went on, and which grew into a titanic pride."[1] In those years, Scriabin expressed his liking for a comparatively small number of composers, such as Chopin, Liszt, and Wagner (he was much more reserved when it came to Beethoven and Bach). There is no record of the young composer's attitude towards Tchaikovsky, whose powerful influence dominated the young musicians of Moscow and to a lesser extent those of St. Petersburg at the time, although the early and the later works of Scriabin undoubtedly bear traces of Tchaikovsky's impact. In the early 1900s, just as he was coming into the prime of his career, Scriabin's spiritual aspirations were closely linked to his philosophical quests. The young musician devoured scholarly literature and was particularly fascinated by idealistic philosophies; he was increasingly carried away by the desire to introduce a philosophical component into music. From that time on his friends and admirers were not limited to musicians—there was, for instance, Trubetzkoy, a professor at the Moscow University, who played a significant role in the composer's philosophical quests.

Scriabin soon abandoned his teaching career at the Moscow Conservatory and the music classes at the Yekaterinin Institute (Rachmaninoff and Goldenweiser also taught there). Wishing to concentrate to the utmost on his composing, he left Moscow and went abroad for several years (1903-1909). The composer retreated into his own artistic world, and his attitude to the great masters of the past took on a peculiar "eclecticism." Wagner interested him primarily because of his search for a "synthetic art" (poetry, music, drama), although the music of certain scenes from Wagner's operas still fascinated him. What attracted Scriabin to Liszt was the Hungarian composer's personality, his devotion to great aesthetic and philosophical ideals. His former enthusiasm for Chopin was all but gone. He spoke extremely critically of Debussy and Richard Strauss. Among Russian composers, he singled out Mussorgsky for his original talent. But it was apparently Rimsky-Korsakov who was closest to him; his work had much in common with Scriabin's—the poetic loftiness of images, the picturesque wealth of sound and "color," and the artistry of musical form. According to his contemporaries, Scria-

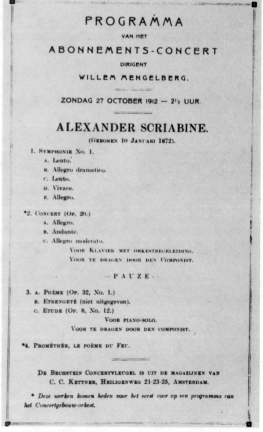

Program of a 1912 concert of Scriabin's works with Willem Mengelberg conducting.

bin was in fact quite indifferent to "somebody else's" music, and it is noteworthy that as early as the 1890s Rimsky-Korsakov mentioned Scriabin's "apathy" regarding the works of other composers.[2]

It was at this time that Scriabin's works became increasingly acclaimed and popular. Many eminent musicians of Russia and Western Europe performed and popularized Scriabin's works: Koussevitzky, Ziloti, Blumenfeld, Cooper, and Saradiev, as well as such famous Western conductors as Nikisch, Mengelberg, Wood, and Fried. The circle of the composer's acquaintances broadened and some of them became his friends (for example, Koussevitzky, who was also the publisher of Scriabin's works for several years). During the 1906-1907 season Scriabin toured the United States, playing his piano compositions, while Altschuler, his friend of conservatory days who had since moved overseas, conducted his symphonic works. Scriabin was an unparalleled performer of his own piano music, but other pianists popularized it as well, such as Vera Scriabin (the composer's first wife), Buyukli, Igumnov, Goldenweiser, and Hofmann. It is known that a piano concerto by Scriabin was performed with the composer at the keyboard and Rachmaninoff as conductor. After the composer's death Rachmaninoff appeared with a program of Scriabin's piano works. In the last(the Moscow) period of his life (after 1909), Scriabin mixed socially with very few people, although he was visited by many—not only musicians, but also writers, painters, and those who were not in any sense professionally connected with art. Not all of them shared their host's artistic and philosophical interests, but they all admired his music. Composers Krein and Akimenko, pianists Goldenweiser and Dobrowen, his former student Nemenov-Lunz, violinist Mogilevsky, music critics Gunst and Sabaneyev, and Zhilayev, an admirer of his music and later an eminent Moscow musical figure, were all frequent visitors. Scriabin befriended symbolist poets Ivanov, Baltrushaitis, Balmont, and Briusov (he was a close friend of the first two); his friendship with artist Leonid Pasternak, which started in the early 1900s, never ceased. In those years Scriabin toured Russia a great deal (in the spring of 1910 he went on a concert tour with the Koussevitzky orchestra along the Volga river) and also made trips abroad (to England in particular). The composer cherished a plan of visiting India—the home of the philosophy which was of special interest to him at the time; he also nurtured ideas of synthetic musical and mystical "rites" (*L'Acte préalable, Mystery*), and wrote his last piano sonatas and pieces. His many activities—concert appearances, preparation of completed works for publication, correspondence and meetings with publishers and all kinds of people in the music world—were combined with enormous inner concentration on creative ideas; the composer lived mainly in the atmosphere of his own music, his own artistic and philosophic quests.

Certain facts of Scriabin's musical life make it possible to distinguish both the consistency of his artistic path and the special place he occupied in Russia's musical life.

Scriabin and his friend, the Lithuanian poet Baltrushaitis, in 1913.

Emil Cooper (1877-1960), the first to perform *The Poem of Ecstasy* in Moscow.

Arthur Nikisch (1855-1922), Hungarian conductor and composer.

Vsevolod Buyukli (1873-1920), pianist, Scriabin's fellow student at the Conservatory. He was the first to perform Scriabin's Third Sonata.

Konstantin Igumnov (1873-1948), pianist, professor at the Moscow Conservatory, one of the best interpreters of Scriabin's works.

Scriabin was endowed with that "unique spirituality and fire" which Miaskovsky also found in Beethoven and Tchaikovsky, but in the compositions of his older contemporary it was more condensed and "inspired."[3] Scriabin's music reveals "the human being to the human being," affirms the power of reason and of creative will, the unlimited possibilities of knowledge of the world and of spiritual reality. The idea it conveys is the triumph of beauty and good, the omnipotence of the artist who is able to transform the "face of life."[4] The composer's conviction that it was possible to achieve this illusory aim, which he considered to be *his* mission as a musician, a human being, and a thinker, explains the prevalence of the festive and joyous element in his music. It appears as a starting point, in the form of a peculiar "presentiment," and also as a generalized, final statement of the composer's sense of life.

Scriabin's works contain not only exultant emotions, not only rhapsodic contemplation of the ideal—his music also brims with great activity and aspiration, along with "stormy" emotions, the pathos of struggle and overcoming.

But tragic collisions do not characterize Scriabin's music in the same sense as they do that of many other composers (such as Beethoven, Chopin, Tchaikovsky, Rachmaninoff). Tragedy— struggle ending in death—is not a feature of his music because it was alien to the general current of his thought.[5]

He used to explain many of his compositions as the implementation in music, through changing psychological states (what might be called "musical pictures of an artist's soul," of the process of creating a beautiful sunny world—a kingdom of unlimited joy, spiritual freedom and supreme tension of creative forces (ecstasy). In the successive, "through-composed" motion of musical images, the decisive role is played by the transformation of light and fragile lyricism—dreams of the ideal—into active and ecstatic heroic spirit, exulting in a goal achieved. This transformation of the "utmost refined" into the "utmost grandiose" (as the composer himself used to say) is attained via the expansive development of the flying themes and, most important, by repeated affirmation of the heroic and passionate element (will-power and self-assertion). We feel that Gorky's famous aphorism, "*Man—how proud it sounds*," may to a certain extent be compared to Scriabin's heroics. After all, the heroes of Gorky's early romantic stories appeared in Russian literature in the same historical period as Scriabin's "hero" did. This speaks for the deep national roots, as well as contemporary spirit, of the composer's art.

We have already mentioned that Scriabin's compositions were in harmony with the era of the first Russian revolution. In this sense the composer's work is remarkable. It appeared and flourished on the crest of the "romantic wave" that arose in the art of Russia at the time—in literature, music, and painting—and became a reflection of the contemporary social atmosphere, being born of a presentiment of the imminent radical changes in the political and spiritual spheres of life. According to Alexander

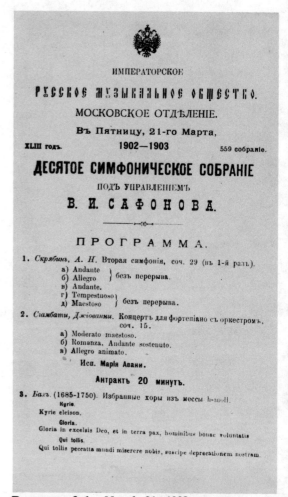

Program of the March 21, 1903 concert, conducted by Safonov, in which Scriabin's Second Symphony was first performed in Moscow.

Blok, the characteristic features of the "new romanticism" were a soaring festiveness of art, "new forms of appreciation," an absolutism of ethical aspirations, and a firm belief in the accessibility of the supreme ideal. "Life is worth living," the poet used to say, "only if one is prepared to make unlimited demands of life: either everything or nothing; to expect the unexpected; to believe, not in 'what does not exist,' but in what should exist."[6] Seeing romanticism as not purely an aesthetic and literary phenomenon, but above all a *socio-psychological* phenomenon, he wrote that romanticism was an "avid urge to live a life ten times as intense, and to build such a life."[7] In other words, Blok considered romanticism to be the artistic attitude of the revolutionary epoch as a whole. Blok's concept of his time is, no matter what we may think of it in scientific terms, undoubtedly related to the problem of the timeliness of Scriabin's work as a phenomenon of Russian life at the turn of the century. It is as if Blok were speaking specifically of Scriabin's music, imbued with living energy, with striving for an ideal and great festive joy. All these are features of romanticism which appear not only in Scriabin, but also in a far broader sense in Russian art at the beginning of our century—the revolutionary heroic era in the country's history.[8] Scriabin's following statement is oft-quoted: "My art in fact presupposes the necessity of revolution."[9] But he also emphasized that the objective of his art was purely spiritual, that it was intended to achieve unlimited *freedom of art*. This is what Scriabin wrote in one of his letters in the spring of 1906: "The political revolution in Russia in its present form and the upheaval of which I dream have nothing to do with each other, although this revolution, no doubt, like any other form of social discontent, brings nearer the desired moment. To use the word 'upheaval' is a mistake. What I want is not *the realization of anything whatsoever*, but the boundless upsurge of creativity that will arise because of my art."[10]

The links between Scriabin's music and the historical situation that gave birth to it are not in the least straightforward or mirror images. "Scriabin's work was his time expressed in sounds. But when the temporary and transient is expressed by a great artist, it acquires eternal meaning and becomes eternal," wrote Plekhanov. At the same time Plekhanov explained that Scriabin conveyed a very subjective, intellectualized reverberation of the revolutionary epoch—through the "temperament and attitude of an idealist and mystic."[11] What Plekhanov was alluding to were the composer's philosophical ideas which gave a very peculiar coloring to the music and poetic images in many of his compositions. Scriabin's dreams about the impact of *his* art on life around him and, in this connection, the philosophical basis of his work, as well as his "messianic" attitude towards his own creative work, all developed under the influence of solipsism—the idealist/subjectivist conception which maintains that the outer world is nothing but a product of individual consciousness. The composer was fascinated by this philosophical doctrine in the 1900s (as his letters and diaries show), but later abandoned it.[12]

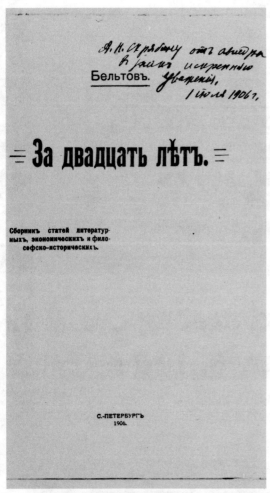

Title page of *Over Twenty Years*, a collection of essays on literature, economics, history, and philosophy by Plekhanov (under the pen name of Beltov), inscribed "To A.N. Scriabin from the author, as a token of sincere respect."

Detroit Symphony

...Orchestra

Third Concert

19th Season

HUGO KALSOW, Director
WM. YUNCK, Concert-Meister
MISS LILLIAN GOVE, Accompanist
FRITZ KALSOW, Manager

—SOLOISTS—

ALEXANDER SCRIABINE
Piano Soloist

MRS. FREDERIC M. BROWN
Soprano-Soloist

MISS RUBY PRATT
Accompanist

Light Guard Armory

Wednesday eve. Mar. 6, 1907

The Concert will begin promptly at 8:15 Standard.
Carriages may be ordered at 9:45.

Seats can be secured at Grinnell Bros.' Music Store, 223 Woodward Ave., Mar. 5th and 6th from 9 a. m. to 5:30 p. m. ♣ ♣ ♣

The management respectfully request the Subscribers to be in their seats before the beginning of the program. ♣ ♣ ♣

Conductor Nikolai Malko (1883-1961), one of the many prominent enthusiasts of Scriabin's music.

← **Placard for Scriabin's Detroit recital.**

Scriabin's beliefs necessitated the social limitations of the rebelliousness and heroism in his music. This explains the contradiction between his universal and all-embracing (hence, democratic) artistic aspirations and his specific, elitist musical and philosophic images. It also explains the great difference between Scriabin the philosopher and Scriabin the musician. In terms of philosophy, he did not create any original doctrine (although in his letters one often comes across such statements as "my main idea," "my teaching," etc.). His opinions—and we can judge them by his recorded statements—characterize Scriabin as a dreamer and poet, but definitely not a scientist.[13] His philosophical views and ideas, his literary-philosophic symbolism (the metaphorical concept of mystical "free play of the spirit," "flame," etc.) fertilized his musical and poetic fantasy and molded its general direction, but at the same time were not quite in harmony with the music itself. It is noteworthy that the program text of the *The Poem of Ecstasy* was written in verse and published *separately* from the score; besides, the conductors and performers were given special instructions: "I would like you to refer to the pure music first."[14] The so-called programs of Scriabin's works were in fact commentaries to *already composed* pieces and were written not by the author, but by others (apparently by his second wife Tatiana Schloezer and her brother Boris Schloezer), although authorized by the composer. Many musicians considered the program commentaries an unnecessary if not undesirable addition to Scriabin's music which impeded understanding of the works. The then-eminent critic Kashkin made a special point of this. These inner collisions in Scriabin's work became even more evident in his last years, after the *The Poem of Ecstasy.*

Despite the striking peculiarity of Scriabin's individuality as thinker and artist, in musical and stylistic terms his work is an historically determined and quite characteristic phenomenon of Russian culture at the turn of the century. It has already been mentioned that his music is extremely romantic. It should be underlined that this romanticism is expressed as an emotional and lyrical, and hence a rather restricted, artistic reflection of the social atmosphere of the time. In this sense Scriabin is much like Rachmaninoff and Medtner, Blok and Vrubel, and to a certain degree like the young Gorky. But typical of Scriabin is his special preception of reality—one might call it a "personal" form of response, an inimitable combination of titanic force and fine, dainty artistic expression.

Scriabin's attention is, in effect, focused on but one aspect of reality, the poetic, to which he gives a very special idealized interpretation. His music recreates the rich and complicated world of an artistically gifted individual whose "spiritual life" is highly exceptional and who is endowed with an acute sense of the good and the beautiful. In Scriabin's music, phenomena of the outer world appear in pantheistic and symbolic images—sea and forest; the night sky with the scintillating magic of the stars; the aerial ocean of day and its dazzling ruler, the Sun; the element of fire.

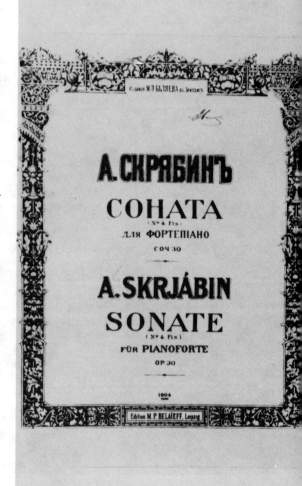

Scriabin's Fourth Sonata. Cover of the Belaieff edition.

Everything assumes in his music a special, grandiose significance —as an expression of the sublimity of the universe, as symbols of the flaming soul and heart, of human creative power.

The fantastic occupies a special place in Scriabin's music, but not in terms of romanticism's traditional folk myths and legends, fairy-tales and *bylinas* (epic folk poems), or the infernal images of hell. The "satanic" (poem Op.36) or "devilish" (the Ninth Sonata) are very rare; a world of bright poetic and philosophic imagination reigns supreme. The illusory and ephemeral ideal required a special form of embodiment, the peculiar hypnosis of a magic dream. Hence, an extraordinary, "super-romantic" strain in the music's emotional pitch. Scriabin's musical dramaturgy of "transformation" has its roots in the aesthetics of romanticism; the same is true of the composer's aspiration for synthetic forms of art—for a new "all-art." However, quests for new ways of amalgamating the arts were very characteristic (although solutions were different) of 20th century culture, Russian included. There is the "musical," "coloristic" poetry of symbolism; Chiurlionis' "musical painting"; Stravinsky's synthetic music and drama forms; and, last but not least, the merging of musical, plastic, and pictorial elements by Meyerhold and Tairov.

Links with the romantic tradition are clearly seen in Scriabin's inclination towards the lyrical instrumental miniature with, as in Chopin, much inner content, and towards the piano and symphonic poem genre; it can also be seen in the renewal of "pure" instrumentalism on a programmatic basis. The romantic origins of the composer's style are also felt in the qualities of the musical language—in the nature of the melodious and declamatory themes, in the character of the harmonic expression and coloring, and in the sphere of timbre, texture and other expressive means. None of these stylistic links overshadows the novelty of Scriabin's style. What was familiar and well known already appears in his early works in a new capacity. As Boris Pasternak neatly emphasized, "Using the methods of his forerunners, Scriabin at the very beginning of his career renewed the feeling of the music."[15]

The historical succession of Scriabin's work, as far as 19th century Russian music is concerned, is quite natural. Scriabin's roots can be found in the lyrical side of it, in the philosophical and aesthetical aspects of the music of Tchaikovsky and Rimsky-Korsakov, Taneyev, and to a certain extent Liadov. Scriabin is close to Tchaikovsky in terms of musical psychologism, romantically ardent emotional expression, and lyrical ("monolog" according to Sollertinsky) symphonic thinking. As in Tchaikovsky, the ebb and flow of the inner tension are depicted in the flexible, expressive movements of melodic themes, in the wave-like character of the development of the musical thought, and in its rush towards the climax. But in Scriabin's music, these processes are more concentrated and impulsive, and span less "musical time." This "compressed" dramaturgy of dynamic intensification is particularly typical of the composer's works of the 1900s. Another distinctive feature of his compositions is his quite

The Seventh Piano Sonata. Autograph.

limited (as compared to Tchaikovsky's) use of genre sources, and their veiled and "unreal" interpretation.

A feature shared with Rimsky-Korsakov is his quiet meditative lyricism colored by a "sense of nature." Lazy and somnolent undulations of the sound mass, prolonged organ points in the lower layer of the orchestral texture, plagal harmonic coloring, and the pentatonic color of the short melodic phrases—all these features of Scriabin's music undoubtedly conjure up associations with the lyrical poetic pages of the scores of his older contemporary. The "Korsakovism" can also be felt in some of Scriabin's lyrical and hymn episodes—coming from the soul of a musician and poet, they are filled with a sweet feeling of merging with Nature ("birds singing" in the middle of the slow part of the Third Symphony; the beautiful B Major Prelude from Op.16). In Scriabin's later compositions, there are parallels with Rimsky-Korsakov in fantastic images—either cold and "lifeless" in their somber torpidity (the beginning of the Ninth Sonata), or shining brightly with warm and colorful patches of sun (the Tenth Sonata).[16]

One cannot fail to notice a certain parallel between Scriabin and Taneyev. No matter how different the two composers' music is, their works are founded on a similar inclination toward a lofty philosophic concept, on the desire to implement in music the human will, to depict the rich and complex inner world of a single hero. In Scriabin's work this world is imbued with subjective attitudes and passionate emotion; in Taneyev's, with objective and rational thinking, with a "sobriety" of feeling.[17]

A great deal has been said about Scriabin's stylistic links to Western composers: they are easily heard in the works of Chopin, Liszt, and Wagner; but the artistic independence of the Russian composer should not be forgotten. This is revealed in his specific choice and *enrichment* of the artistic achievements of romantics of other lands. Scriabin developed the "pure" lyrical element of Chopin's music, its psychological nature—but not the genre and objective side, nor the national epic folklore figurativeness. Nor did Scriabin take up Chopin's cantilena, although he enriched the Chopin *instrumental* melodics. The whimsical metric-rhythmical breath of Chopin's music, its "rubato" nature, which had never been notated, was more individualized and even "written-in" by Scriabin. In particular, he gave freedom to the polyphonic "life" of voices, and a peculiar recherché quality to the piano coloring.

Liszt's oratorical pathos and the orchestral nature of his piano compositions were harmoniously interlaced in the Scriabin style. But the pathetic images of the Russian composer's music have none of Liszt's somewhat superficial pompousness and unwieldy "materiality" of sound. They are more inspired and filled with inner flame. Scriabin achieved power of sound without sacrificing the transparency and lightness of the musical tissue; it never became cumbersome and retained its mobility and "flying" quality because of the fine melodization of the texture and the chord repetitions which created in finales a "beating" effect through the resounding of the chord masses. Scriabin developed his program-

The program of the January 31, 1909 concert, conducted by Blumenfeld, in which Scriabin's Fifth Piano Sonata and *The Poem of Ecstasy* were premiered, with the composer himself at the piano.

matic principle on the basis of *his own* philosophical themes—bypassing the literary, poetic, and folklore roots typical of Liszt and other romantics.

Scriabin was also independent in relation to Wagner. Of the entire wealth of the great German master's imagery, Scriabin "chose" only the "Graal," which was so close to him because it was "ideal" in its purity and fragility, and Wagner's condensed and sensual lyrics of "languor." But Scriabin gradually transformed Wagner's sensual lyrics into something "ethereal" and "starry," while the languorous images lost their amorous significance and became an expression of *spiritual* striving for an ideal dream.

In his means of musical expression, and above all in his modal thinking, Scriabin proceeded from the late romantic style, from Wagner's harmonic language of the *Tristan and Isolde* epoch. These sources were evident in his compositions of the first decade of the 20th century. By the middle of the decade, his individual style was fully crystallized. Scriabin went his own way, and his innovative thinking played an important role in the renewal of musical language that was characteristic of the beginning of the century.[18]

It is necessary to mention the relationship of Scriabin's work to stylistic tendencies such as impressionism, expressionism and symbolism, which emerged as the new artistic trends in Russian cultural life and in European art at the turn of the century. It is not always possible clearly to determine the analogies and "similarities" between Scriabin's music and the aesthetics and stylistics of those trends, although one often comes across certain "convergences," primarily in the works of the last ten or twelve years of his life. Much more evident are the contiguities of Scriabin's art with symbolism because of the great significance he attributed to philosophic and poetic symbolics, to the mysterious and "uncognizable" nature of certain images, and to the metaphorical meaning of certain abstract themes ("the theme of reason," "the theme of Prometheus") or representational themes ("sparkling fountain"). Another feature which brings Scriabin close to symbolism is his search for the "supra-real" ideal, his aspiration for pure "spirituality" in art. But this does not at all mean that the composer can be considered a typical and complete "symbolist" in music, for the Romantic tradition was still the basis of his art. Certain stylistic features of his works, and details of musical exposition create a superficial similarity with impressionism and expressionism. With impressionism, because of the peculiar, fleeting sound-coloring, the fine play of light and shade, picturesque half-tones, the capturing of hardly perceptible motions of the soul. With expressionism, because of the feverish anxiety of the music, its emotional instability, fluctuations between extreme excitement and psychological immobility. But in fact, the essential aesthetic principles of both these trends had little in common with the music of Scriabin—such as the impressionists' pictorial approach to reality, the elements of hedonism in their aesthetics, their very musical (harmonic) language. Alien

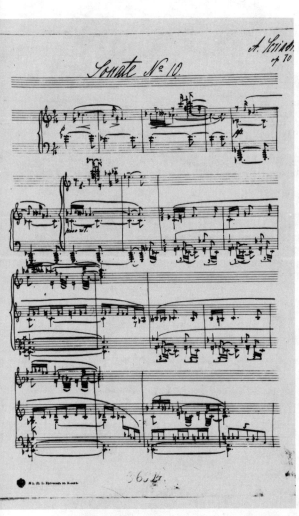

The Tenth Sonata. First page of the manuscript.

F. Liszt.

Program of the February 1, 1913 concert, conducted by Sir Henry
Wood, which included the English premiere of Scriabin's *Prometheus*.

to Scriabin was also the expressionists' pessimistic sense of life, their desire to depict a sick, "torn" consciousness, and their rejection of classical musical forms.

Scriabin's historical role in the development of symphonic and piano music is indeed great. In the history of symphonic music, three of his monumental scores, above all the Third Symphony, which Scriabin called the *The Divine Poem*, form one of the summits in the evolution of the genre. The traditions of Beethoven's heroic symphonism, of Tchaikovsky's lyrical and psychological "symphonic dramas," and of Taneyev's philosophic and lyrical instrumental cycles (both orchestral and chamber) were all continued by Scriabin. *The Poem of Ecstasy* and *The Poem of Fire* (*Prometheus*), which came as a logical development of the principles of the composer's symphonic dramaturgy (the tendency to close the cycle into a one-movement poem), are fundamentallly different from Liszt's poems both in content and in compositional form. Scriabin's works are founded not on "condensed cyclic recurrence" as are Liszt's, but on a "renewed sonata style," for they are based on the one-movement sonata allegro. In *Prometheus*, the composer enriched the symphonic poem with features of other genres, such as cantata (wordless chorus), instrumental concerto (piano solo), and sound-color symphony (the part of light).

In his mature orchestral works, Scriabin created his own complete and graphic symphonic style in two versions: the one-movement and the cyclic. In the dramaturgy of the Third Symphony, the similarities and the differences between Scriabin's and Tchaikovsky's symphonic principles become evident. What brings the first movement of this symphony and Tchaikovsky's symphonic monodramas together is the wealth and ramification of the contrasts, the wave type of development, and the complicated dialectics of the emotional collisions. But the difference lies in the supremacy and the all-pervading significance of the heroic idea, the importance of self-assertion and not fatalism. The principal leit-motif is interpreted as an absolute; it does not figure (unlike in Tchaikovsky) in the collisions of struggle, it is beyond the panorama of conflict, it rises above it. Developing the principles of the monodramaturgy (monothematicism) of Tchaikovsky's and Taneyev's symphonic cycles, Scriabin achieves even closer musical unity in a large composition, he emphasizes the common features of the movements through the continuous transition from one to another. Hence, in the Third Symphony, the cycle turns into a poem. In *Prometheus*, Scriabin creates a new type of symphonic dramaturgy: the conflict of antagonistic images recedes, and is replaced by a recurring contrast (juxtaposition of episodes that are at opposite poles in terms of their expressive nature and musical content). The accelerating shifts of contrasts create the "dynamics of over-excitement" typical of the late Scriabin and turn into a kind of "gigantic pulsation" (as Lunacharsky put it). It makes the musical composition "vibrate," leading to the triumph of ecstasy.

Transition from a many-movement form to concise one-

***Désir.* Autograph.**

30

movement composition is also typical of Scriabin's sonatas. As with his symphonic music, it is stipulated by the change of the nature of the musical images: the lyrical and dramatic program (in the First Sonata, it is autobiographic) is replaced, starting with the Fourth Sonata, by a philosophic program; this is accompanied by changes in the aesthetics and the style of music. With Scriabin, the piano sonata genre evolved beyond his symphonic music. In the last sonatas (the Ninth and the Tenth) and in the final opus numbers of the piano poems, preludes, and études, certain new tendencies appeared: a turn to more objective images with genres more clearly defined, to a more integral dramaturgy—in particular intensification through ostinato (the poem *Vers la flamme*)—or one of dynamic conflict (the Ninth Sonata). But these features were no longer reflected in Scriabin's later symphonic music; its evolution abruptly halted at the stage of his working out of a new concept—even more extraordinary than that of *Prometheus*—, the synthetic, symphonic, and vocal *L'Acte préalable*. Scriabin was the first Russian composer to place piano music at the center of his creative work. It was he who gave a special and independent importance to the Russian piano sonata, and raised it to the level of symphonic and music-drama genres. The path Scriabin blazed was continued by his younger contemporaries, the outstanding composers and pianists Medtner and Prokofiev, who created new types of Russian sonata, with no resemblance to Scriabin's, either in terms of contents or style. Scriabin's lesser piano forms happened to be a peculiar continuation of the chamber tradition of piano music, both Western and Russian. At the same time that Scriabin's first preludes and études, mazurkas and impromptus appeared, Rachmaninoff wrote his first piano pieces. But Scriabin established his own style, with a transparent and colorful manner of writing that made the most of the instrument's expressive and timbre resources, and a finely chiseled form.[19] The piano poem genre created by the composer occupies an intermediate position between his preludes and the one-movement sonatas; many of the poems have program titles ["Satanic Poem" ("Poème satanique"), "Vers la flamme" (Towards the flame), "Poème ailé" ("Winged poem"), "Masques" (Masks"), "Etrangeté" ("An Oddity"), etc.]. Scriabin has taken his rightful place in the history of music alongside Chopin, Schumann, and Rachmaninoff as one of the great "romantics of the piano."

The creator of *The Poem of Ecstasy*, of the Fourth and the Fifth Sonatas is one of those whose music cannot be imitated: he was too unique, his artistic quests too extraordinary, his musical style too individual. Immediately after their appearance, his compositions stirred a heated controversy. Scriabin was treated differently by the older and the younger generations of musicians, although there was no unanimity in either of the "camps." Stasov was extremely impressed by Scriabin's compositions, whereas Cui was bitterly hostile. While recognizing Scriabin's tremendous musical talent, Rimsky-Korsakov was wary about the basic trend of his work. "Scriabin, a star of the first magnitude, is

Masque. Autograph.

Mark Meychik (1880-1950), pianist, the first performer of Scriabin's Fifth Sonata in Moscow.

Moscow, 11 Nikolo-Peskovsky Lane (now Vakhtangov Street). Scriabin
lived in this his last apartment (at present, the Scriabin State Museum)
since October 1912.

somewhat affected, ostentatious, and conceited," wrote Rimsky-Korsakov in his reminiscences.[20] Glazunov, Liadov and Taneyev accepted his music (but not his aesthetic concepts) with warm approval but with strong reservations, taking exception to some of his works.

Nevertheless, between 1900 and 1910 Scriabin's music grew more and more popular, and he became the idol of many musicians, especially the younger ones. Miaskovsky was enthusiastic about his music, and so was the young Prokofiev (although not to the same extent). Articles and reviews written by the eminent music critics of the pre-revolutionary period, such as Miaskovsky and Karatygin, Engel and Gunst, Sabaneyev and Saminsky, attest to the lively interest that Scriabin's work aroused in his contemporaries. The influence of Scriabin's style can be traced in some of Prokofiev's early piano miniatures, in Miaskovsky's compositions from 1910 to 1920, and in works by young composers of the pre- and post-revolutionary years (Gnessin, Alexandrov, Feinberg, etc.). Critics also find "scriabinisms" in the works of some foreign composers (such as Karlowicz and Szymanowski). In the young Soviet Russia, Scriabin's music took on a special significance and a new perspective. It was perceived as a reflection of the romantic, rebellious spirit of the Revolution, as a declaration of its liberating and creative pathos. Lunacharsky was an enthusiastic advocate of Scriabin's heritage, and his brilliant articles furnished a sociological analysis of the philosophical and poetic content of Scriabin's music. Promoting performances of Scriabin's works on anniversaries of revolutionary events and on other special occasions and festivities held by the Soviet State, Lunacharsky often appeared as a lecturer at concerts, where he would explain how the composer's music was shaped by the revolutionary era, and draw a parallel between his music and the music of Beethoven. Scriabin's name was on the list of the outstanding figures of the revolution, of science, and of art that was compiled for memorial monuments in their honor in the plan approved by Lenin.

A serious study of Scriabin's life and work to provide an objective scholarly evaluation of the brilliant Russian composer's heritage and to determine his historical significance was already begun prior to the revolution. The first collection of biographical and research articles about Scriabin appeared in the double issue (Nos. 4 and 5) of the magazine *Musical Contemporary* in 1916. The monographic essay "Scriabin" by Karatygin, the brief but meaningful statements by Miaskovsky in his article "Tchaikovsky and Beethoven" and in his "St. Petersburg letters," and evaluations by Igor Glebov (Boris Asafiev) in the article "Three deaths" in the *Muzika (Music)* magazine are also of great interest.

Studies of Scriabin's music flourished after the Revolution. The publication of primary sources (the composer's diaries, his philosophical notes, drafts of the libretto to the opera which was not completed, texts of *The Poem of Ecstasy* and *L'Acte préalable*, as well as manuscript scores was a milestone. Other landmarks of Soviet "scriabiniana" should be noted: the anniversary collection

The Fifth Sonata. Cover of the author's edition.

published on the 25th anniversary of his death, in 1940 (reminiscences and research), works by Alschwang, an analysis of Scriabin's historical significance in Asafiev's book *Russian Music: the 19th and the Early 20th Century*, and finally the first extensive and carefully annotated collection of the composer's letters with a commentary (compiled and edited by Kashperov, introductory article by Asmus).

Also very important, as far as studies of the composer's heritage are concerned, was the opening of a state museum in his last residence, and the accumulation there, and at the Glinka State Central Museum of Musical Culture, of his music and literary manuscript materials.

Scriabin's music is heard extensively on the Soviet concert stage. Among the older generation of musicians and Scriabin admirers are conductors Golovanov, Malko, Nebolsin, and Mravinsky, and pianists Neuhaus, Feinberg, and particularly Sofronitzky, who was a magnificent and undoubtedly the finest (except for the composer himself) interpreter of Scriabin's works.[21] Later, younger generations of Soviet musicians brought forth many talented and fine "scriabinists." In recent years, Scriabin's music has been more often performed, and has become increasingly popular with the public. The 100th anniversary of the composer's birth was a veritable festival of Soviet music, and did much to highlight the never-dwindling artistic significance of Scriabin's work.

This publication presents a consecutive record of Scriabin's life and work, with the material systematized in accordance with his artistic evolution. There are several "chapters" in the album. The first chapter is about the composer's childhood, his formative years as a musician, his studies at the Moscow Conservatory, and his first experiences as a composer (1872-1891). The second deals with the first decade of his independent music career and the compositions of those years (1892-1902). The third embraces the five years between 1903 and 1908, which can be called a "heroic epoch" in Scriabin's creative life. The Fourth Sonata, Third Symphony, *The Poem of Ecstasy*, and Fifth Sonata—all written at that time—form a "heroic tetralogy" which is considered the acme of the composer's work. The fourth chapter is about the last period of Scriabin's life (1909-1915). The fifth describes the place of Scriabin's music in Soviet musical life: the new social significance of his music, and its "encounters" with an unusually expanded and democratic audience; here we also see a "panorama" of Scriabin's works in concert and the outstanding Soviet performers who are true friends of Scriabin's music; finally come materials on the Scriabin State Museum and the celebration of the 100th anniversary of the composer's birth. This book features pictures of Scriabin and also of relatives, friends, musicians, and other people with whom he had either friendly or professional, artistic, and business relations. The illustrations include many autographs, concert programs, editions of Scriabin's works, and other documents pertaining to his life and career. There are also pictures of the places where the composer lived or

Program of Scriabin's 1914 recital in London.

Mikhail Tabakov (1877-1956), the first and best interpreter of the trumpet solo part in *The Poem of Ecstasy*.

Anatoly Alexandrov (b. 1888), an eminent pianist and composer whose style was greatly influenced by Scriabin.

which he visited; these materials provide a better idea of the environment in which the composer lived and worked.

Many statements by contemporaries, illustrious Scriabin scholars, and interpreters of his music appear in the text; thus, "voices" of those who were the first to hear and appreciate his work become a part of the story. Some information—biographical details, facts about the people with whom the composer mixed, about the writing and the performance of certain works—is added or specified in the commentaries.

Documentary materials from the Scriabin State Museum were placed at the publishers' disposal by the director of the Museum.

The Poem of Ecstasy. **Cover of the Belaieff edition.**

Московское Филармоническое Общество.

Въ субботу, 10-го декабря,

въ Большомъ залѣ Россійскаго Благороднаго Собранія

ПЯТОЕ СИМФОНИЧЕСКОЕ СОБРАНІЕ,

подъ управленіемъ С. В. Рахманинова.

съ участіемъ А. Н. Скрябина.

Правленіе Общества покорнѣйше проситъ:

Во время исполненія музыкальныхъ номеровъ
не входить и не выходить изъ зала и громко
не разговаривать.

Program of a concert in which Scriabin performed.

Notes to Preface

[1] J. Engel, "Scriabin: A Biographical Essay," *Musical Contemporary*, book 4/5, (St. Petersburg: 1916), p. 32.

[2] See V.V. Yastrebzev, *Nikolai Andreyevitch Rimsky-Korsakov: Reminiscences* (Leningrad, 1959), vol. 1, p. 269.

[3] See N. Miaskovsky, *Collection of Materials in Two Volumes* (Moscow: 1964), vol. 2, pp. 58, 61.

[4] This idea was already typical of the 19th century romantics, such as Liszt and Wagner. The elevated idea of the mission of art and the role of the artist was also reflected in the work of Rimsky-Korsakov, in his image-embodiments of "kind beauty" and "wise beauty."

[5] One exception was the finale of the First Sonata (Funeral March).

[6] Alexander Blok, *Complete Works in 8 Volumes* (Moscow-Leningrad: 1962), vol. 6, p. 14.

[7] Ibid, p. 367.

[8] In a letter to Chekhov, Gorky wrote that the craving for the heroic, festive, ideal, and beautiful was the spirit of the time. (See M. Gorky, *Complete Works in 30 Volumes* [Moscow-Leningrad: 1954], vol. 28, p. 113). An interesting fact is that this kind of romanticism was not at all peculiar to late romantic Western music of the turn of the century or to the expressionism which grew out of it (for example, Mahler and early Schönberg).

[9] See A.N. Drozdov, "Reminiscences of Scriabin," *Soviet Music*, 1946, no. 12, p. 72.

[10] A. Scriabin, *Letters*, compiled and edited by A. Kashperov, (Moscow: 1965), p. 422.

[11] G. Plekhanov, "Letters to Dr. Bogorodsky," *Literature and Aesthetics* (Moscow: 1958), vol. 2, p. 495. See also A. Alschwang, Selected Works in 2 Volumes (Moscow: 1964), vol. 1, p. 176.

[12] For details about Scriabin's philosophical views and their reflection in his work see articles about Scriabin by A. Lunacharsky in the collection *In the Realm of Music* (Moscow: 1968); the collection *Alexander Scriabin (1915-1940): For the 25th anniversary of his death*, (Moscow: 1940); A. Alschwang, *Selected Works in 2 Volumes* (Moscow: 1964, 1965).

A family picture. Three-year-old Alexander Scriabin is in the front row, standing beside his grandmother Ye. Scriabin.

[13] Alluding to Scriabin's acquaintance with Marxism, which did not change his philosophical convictions, R. Plekhanova writes: "He could not stand on solid scientific ground" (see the collection *Alexander Scriabin*, p. 74).

[14] A. Scriabin, *Letters*, p. 491.

[15] B. Pasternak, "About Scriabin and Chopin," *Soviet Music*, Jan. 1967, p. 100.

[16] This link is noted by S. Pavchinsky in his book *Scriabin's Works of the Late Period* (Moscow: 1969).

[17] Another parallel, "Scriabin-Liadov," is also justified. Liadov can be considered Scriabin's precursor in Russian chamber paino music, although it was with Scriabin that fine and specific piano exposition reached its peak. In 1890-1900, Liadov in turn experienced the influence of Scriabin's style (Liadov's piano pieces op. 64: "Grimaces," "Twilight," "Temptation," "Recollection").

[18] Soviet musicologists Yavorsky, Skrebkov, Berkov, Dernov, Khlopov, and Pavchinsky have made a great contribution to the study of Scriabin's musical language. But this issue has not yet been fully solved.

[19] For details about Scriabin's piano style see: S. Feinberg, *Pianism as an Art* (Moscow: 1969).

[20] N. Rimsky-Korsakov, *Complete Works: Literary Works and Correspondence* (Moscow: 1955), vol. I, p. 212.

[21] Eminent Soviet musicians who began playing Scriabin's music while he was still alive are mentioned above.

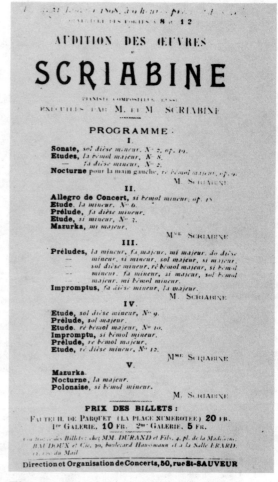

The program of the duo recital by Alexander and Vera Scriabin in the Erard Hall in Paris on January 31, 1898.

"Scriabin. . .is a great seeker of new ways. . .by means of an unprecedented new language he opens up for us extraordinary emotional perspectives that can barely be realized, such heights of spiritual enlightenment that in our opinion he becomes a phenomenon of world-wide significance. . ."[1]

"Scriabin's music is an irrepressible and deeply humane aspiration for freedom, joy and delight. Constant dissatisfaction and tension of all energies accompany each other—and the music continues to exist as a living witness to the best expectations of the epoch when it was an 'explosive,' exciting, and agitated element of culture."[2]

1872-1891
Early Years

Moscow Conservatory

Beginnings as a Composer

Moscow in the 19th Century.

Alexander Scriabin was born in Moscow on January 6, 1872 (December 25, 1871 Julian calendar).

His mother, Lubov Shchetinin, graduated from the St. Petersburg conservatory in 1869, in the class of the famous pianist and teacher Leshetitzky (she had also studied with Anton Rubinstein). She was awarded the Highest Gold Medal, appeared publicly in St. Petersburg and Russian provincial towns, and was a promising concert pianist.

". . . Laroche and Tchaikovsky both spoke to me about Miss Shchetinin, who was at the conservatory at the same time they were, referring to her as the most talented pianist in Leshetitzky's class . . ."

N. Kashkin[3]

Nikolai Scriabin, the composer's father, was abroad most of the time because of his consular service, and saw his son rather infrequently. He entrusted his sister Lubov with the boy's upbringing. Eight years after the death of his first wife, he remarried (to an Italian woman, by the name of Fernández).

Lubov Scriabin loved music and played a great deal, providing the youngster with his first musical impressions. She left reminiscences about Scriabin, extracts of which were published in the book *Alexander Scriabin, 1915-1940: Anthology for the 25th anniversary of the composer's death* (Moscow-Leningrad: 1940).

"Ours was a close, old-fashioned family."

L.A. Scriabin[4]

Lubov Petrovna Scriabin, née Shchetinin (1849-1873), the composer's
mother.

Nikolai Alexandrovich Scriabin (1849-1914), the composer's father.
After graduating from the College of Oriental Languages, he joined the
consular service, and in the last years of his life was the general consul
in Erzurum (Turkey).

Alexander Scriabin in 1879.

Alexander Scriabin with his father in 1882.

"A love of music was born with him in the cradle. . .At the age of three, Sasha (Alexander) used to come up to me and say, 'Auntie, give me a seat.' I knew that he wanted me to put him in front of the piano. . .I helped him sit up on a cushion and he could spend hours at the piano. I would take a book or my needlework and sit beside him, listening to him picking out something with one finger."

L.A. Scriabin[5]

"Rubinstein was amazed by Sasha's musical talent and asked me never to make him play or compose unless he wanted to."

L.A. Scriabin[6]

"He adored nature. . .we often walked in the forest; he always brought along music paper and a pencil, and said that many good ideas came to him during those walks. . ."

L.A. Scriabin[7]

Images of nature were reflected in Scriabin's symphonies and sonatas (the Second, Fourth, and Tenth), in several preludes and other compositions.

Scriabin was in the Cadet Corps school from 1882 to 1889. At his first public appearance he played "Venetian Boat Song" (from *Songs Without Words*) by Mendelssohn, and a Gavotte by Bach. His stepmother used to play those pieces, and he had learned them by ear.

"It happened on the 8th of November, on our school holiday. On that day we had a concert in the evening. . .and suddenly our boisterous and high-spirited crowd saw Sasha on the stage. . . Scriabin's recital ended with wild applause. The cadets were so excited that the tutors and later the director himself had to quiet them down."

L. Limantov
(Scriabin's fellow-student in the Cadet Corps).[8]

In the summer of 1882, Scriabin began to study music on a regular basis. His first outside teachers, prior to joining the Conservatory, were Conus and Taneyev.

". . .That summer I spent in Demianova, near Klin. The Scriabins' dacha was not far away, in Maidanovo I suppose. Once while riding, I happened to find myself at their dacha. I took Alexander away to Demianovo to see what progress he had made in music. I had him sit down in the park under an oak and asked him to write counterpoint."

S. Taneyev[9]

"When he was thirteen, Taneyev suggested that he study with Professor Zverev. Sergei Ivanovitch himself proposed to teach him music theory."

L.A. Scriabin[10]

Zverev, an illustrious Moscow music teacher, taught the junior grades at the Moscow conservatory from 1870 onwards, and in 1883 was appointed professor. Scriabin took piano lessons from him between 1885 and 1887. One of Scriabin's Nocturnes (A-flat major) written at this time was published for the 40th anniversary of the composer's death (it was included in the complete col-

Ballade (1887). The theme of the ***Ballade*** became the basis for the Prelude, Op. 11, No. 4.

lection of Scriabin's piano works).

The image of the dream, so typical of Scriabin's music, and the author's commentary, revealing the content of the music in poetic form, make their first appearance in the youthful *Ballade*.

> Beautiful land,
> And life is different here. . .
> But no place for me. . .
> I hear voices, and see the world of blissful souls. . .
> But do not see her!
> The sounds have faded, and I am as wretched as before,
> I am near a magnificent castle.
> Always the same voice, the same dream.
>
> *Scriabin's text to the* Ballade[11]

The theme of the second movement of the Piano Concerto, Op. 20, completed in 1897, was composed by Scriabin at the age of 15.

"There was to be an evening recital given by the Conservatory students in the Grand Hall of the Nobles' Assembly. Although Sasha was still studying with Zverev, he also had to perform."

L.A. Scriabin[12]

By this time, Scriabin was no longer a student of Zverev; in January 1888 he was admitted to the Conservatory where he studied with Safonov.

"I went to visit Sasha. Found him at home alone. He was sitting in the large room and working. . .Then Sasha came up to the piano and started to play what he had written. . .'What is it you were playing?'—'It's a sonata. . .I have just written it.'"

L. Limantov[13]

The Second Moscow Cadet Corps in Lefortovo which Scriabin attended.

"The compositions of young Scriabin were received with more attention, even enthusiasm, in the household of the Institute physician, Dr. Monighetti. . .The Monighetti family consisted of the father, mother and two daughters. They lived a full, merry, tumultuous life, with many young people coming around. Both sisters, as well as their parents, loved music. . .Scriabin felt at home in their family, and retained a special, warm feeling for them to the end of his life."

J. Engel[14]

Olga Monighetti often gave Scriabin friendly support; she introduced him to the conductor Koussevitzky, who was to become an outstanding interpreter of Scriabin's music and, for several years, his publisher. Olga Monighetti left reminiscences of Scriabin, now kept in the Scriabin State Museum.

In January 1888, Scriabin entered the Moscow Conservatory, where he studied counterpoint under Taneyev and piano under Safonov.

Scriabin studied only introductory counterpoint (austere style) with Taneyev because at that time Taneyev did not teach advanced counterpoint.

Safonov held Scriabin's talents in high esteem and promoted him both as pianist and composer.

"As a pianist, Scriabin made tremendous strides while studying with Safonov. I remember how beautifully he played such pieces

Scriabin in 1887.

Sergei Taneyev (1856-1915), a distinguished composer and outstanding pedagogue, with whom Scriabin studied privately from 1884 to 1888.

Limantov, Scriabin's fellow student at the Cadet Corps.

Olga Monighetti (1869-1952).

as *Allegro de Concert* by Chopin, his first G Minor Ballade, Beethoven's Sonata, Op. 101 in A Major, etc."

M. Presmann[15]

[M.L. Presmann (1870-1941) was Scriabin's fellow-student in the Zverev class. After graduating from the Moscow Conservatory, he worked in Rostov-on-the-Don. Later, he became a professor at the Baku Conservatory, and then director of the Ippolitov-Ivanov Music School in Moscow. His reminiscences, *A Corner of Musical Moscow of the 1880s*, were published in the two-volume collection *Reminiscences of Rachmaninoff* compiled and edited by Z. Apetyan, with commentary and introduction: 4th edition, Moscow, 1974].

"A great deal in his manner was mine. But he had a special diversity of sound, a special, ideally delicate use of the pedal; he had a rare and exceptional gift: his instrument was breathing."

V. Safonov[16]

In 1891-1892, Scriabin studied fugue and free composition with Arensky.

". . .Arensky won neither Scriabin's respect nor his love. Insensitive as he was to a student's individuality, he failed to discern in Scriabin a budding great artist. The relations between teacher and the student became extremely strained, and Scriabin dropped Arensky's composition course."

A. Ossovsky[17]

[A. Ossovsky (1871-1957), a music critic whose articles often appeared in the *Russkaya Muzikalnaya Gazeta (Russian Musical Paper)*, was a professor at the St. Petersburg (Leningrad) Conservatory; he wrote a memoir, *Young Scriabin*—see A. Ossovsky, *Selected Articles and Reminiscences*, Leningrad, 1961.]

Scriabin left the Arensky class after Arensky turned down his request that the free composition course be reduced for him to one year.

"The winter of 1890-1891. . .In the musical circles of Moscow, they were talking about a new, extraordinary musical talent.

It was a regular music-making party. Right in the middle of our performance of. . .the Mozart Trio in E Major, there appeared a slim, thin young man under medium height, with blond hair, a pale face, a slightly turned-up but daintly outlined nose, and a fluffy moustache and beard. It was Scriabin. . .His movements were nervous, jerky and sharp, his demeanor very modest, his manner unassuming. . .Host and guests all entreated Scriabin to play some of his own music. Willingly, without showing off, Scriabin sat down at the piano. It took him but a few moments to enthrall the audience. Even in those early years, Scriabin already possessed his lifelong gift of establishing a psychological contact with audiences from the first chords, of exuding a certain nervous, hypnotic current that one could not resist. Then, as always in the future, he played his own works only: the B-Major Prelude, F-sharp Minor Nocturne, C-sharp Minor Etude, a waltz, and several mazurkas from the collection of pieces which was soon to be published by the Jurgenson Publishing House. Performed by Scriabin, they were like improvisations, as if born

A page from the Monighettis' album, autographed by Scriabin in 1889.

on the spot and still bearing the uncooled ardor of inspiration: there was flight and freedom and whimsy in his playing, there was a breath of freshness and spontaneity. The very sound of the instrument under the magic fingers of his handsome, well-groomed, and small hands was captivating. The performance bore the mark of a unique individuality, of a lofty grace of soul reflected in the grace of form."

A. Ossovsky[18]

". . .During his initial Conservatory years he spent most of the time at home; it was very seldom that we went to a concert. He did not like to go out, and usually his friends came to visit him around tea-time when he took some time off from his diligent studies. In those hours of relaxation Sasha was very cheerful and outgoing, especially when his regular visitors—Avierino, Cherniaev, Rachmaninoff, Levin, Buyukli, Rosenov, and Shor—came. Very often, one could hear them laugh the whole evening through".

L.A. Scriabin[19]

(Levin graduated from the Moscow Conservatory in 1892 and taught piano there from 1902 to 1906.)

In 1892 Scriabin graduated from the Moscow Conservatory piano class with a gold medal. By a special decision of the Conservatory Council, Scriabin's name was inscribed, alongside Taneyev's and Rachmaninoff's, on the Marble Plaque in the foyer of the Minor Hall of the Conservatory (though usually only the names of honors graduates of two Conservatory classes were inscribed on the plaque).

Scriabin's Conservatory graduation diploma.

Vasily Safonov (1852-1918), renowned pianist, conductor, teacher, and, from 1889 to 1905, president of the Moscow Conservatory.

Violinist Nikolai Avierino (1872-1948), one of Scriabin's Conservatory friends.

Alexander Scriabin in 1897.

1892-1902
After Graduation
First Artistic Period

After graduating from the Conservatory, Scriabin began his independent career as a composer and pianist. In 1893, his works were published for the first time by Jurgenson, a leading music publisher (although Scriabin did not receive any royalties).

"On my table I found several proof-sheets from Jurgenson, and a letter saying there have been orders for my waltz from Leipzig, Gmunden and Vienna (three copies from Gmunden). That made me extremely happy, and I shall do my best not to make people wait for the forthcoming issues. Two nocturnes will come out in a week, and perhaps an etude as well. Now I will start trimming up the sonata."

A. Scriabin
(from his letter to Natalia Sekerin,
July 20, 1892)[20]

"In those years. . .Scriabin as an artist lived through a tragic catastrophe. Alexander got it into his head to have a piano competition with his older fellow-student Iosif Levin, who had a phenomenal but purely technical piano gift. Practicing for the duel, Scriabin 'overplayed' his right hand doing Balakirev's *Islamey* and Mozart-Liszt's *Don Giovanni*. The then-eminent diagnostician, Dr. Zakharyin, pronounced the injury incurable."

A. Ossovsky[21]

"The *first* serious failure in my life. The first serious reflection: *a beginning of analysis*. Although I *doubt* the impossibility of recovery, the mood is most gloomy. . .Composing the 1st Sonata with the funeral march."

A. Scriabin[22]

"To become an optimist in the full sense of the word, one must experience and conquer despair."

A. Scriabin[23]

". . .Sasha made his acquaintance with the Sekerin family, which consisted of the mother and two daughters. The younger one was about fifteen—a beautiful, clever, and gifted girl. Alexander became increasingly carried away and was very pleased when finally invited to visit them, which he did twice a week".

L.A. Scriabin[24]

Natalia Sekerin met Scriabin in 1891. They soon became

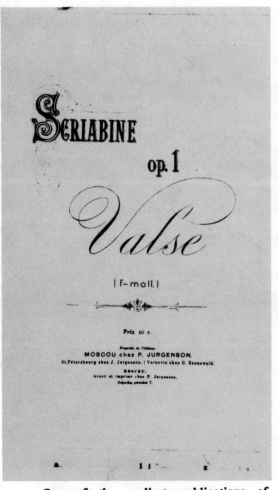

SCRIABINE

op. 1

Valse

(F-moll.)

Prix 40 c.

Propriété de l'éditeur
MOSCOU chez P. JURGENSON.
St.Petersbourg chez J. Jurgenson. | Varsovie chez G. Sennewald.
MOSCOU.
Gravé et imprimé chez P. Jurgenson.

One of the earliest publications of Scriabin's works.

Natalia Sekerin (1877-1958).

Scriabin's Etude Op. 8 No. 12.

XII.

A. Scriàbine. Op. 8 No 12.

Patetico ♩=100-112.

friends and then fell in love. The composer's youthful love was reflected in some of his early works (according to Natalia's sister, in his only romance and several piano pieces). Scriabin made a gift to Natalia Sekerin of his early sonata-fantasy (published later in the Complete Piano Works).

"Stop! What is this insane flight for? Don't you know that even the light that reached you from the star swerved from its path while moving through different spheres. How dare you then, you wretched thing, not be afraid that life will crush you? So it is; but the star is so beautiful, and I love my star so much, that if I do not go on looking at it, if it does not continue to shine for me and I do not strive to reach it, then thought will die, and everything else too. Better for me to be destroyed in a mad effort, but thought will remain and triumph."

A. Scriabin
(from his letter to Natalia Sekerin,
Moscow, May 25, 1893)[25]

"Perhaps you are not attracted by our simple, but heart-felt and melancholic Russian landscape? I can't believe it. How can one not love what is true?"

A. Scriabin
(from a letter to Natalia Sekerin,
Zenino, September 26, 1894)

"At the present moment I am staying with the Safonovs in Kislovodsk. . .The wonderful Caucasian air and the mountains where I go for long walks every day with the kids (it is my destiny to walk with children) have a wholesome effect. . ."

A. Scriabin
(from a letter to Natalia Sekerin,
Kislovodsk, September 27, 1894)

In 1884, Belaieff founded a music publishing house in Leipzig which issued works only by Russian composers, paying them rather princely royalties. In 1885, he organized Russian symphonic concerts and, in 1891, Russian quartet evenings. On all important questions he consulted Rimsky-Korsakov, Liadov, and Glazunov.

Scriabin met Belaieff in the spring of 1894. In 1895, Belaieff became Scriabin's publisher and continued to publish his works until 1907.

". . .Stasov. . .talked about a new rising star—the pianist and composer Scriabin, who played Friday and Saturday (in the afternoon after the rehearsal) at Belaieff's, where he was lodging. Everyone is crazy about him—Rimsky-Korsakov, Liadov, Blumenfeld, Lavrov, and Belaieff (and Stasov, of course)."

N. Findeisen
(from diary, December 26, 1895)[28]

"A great and new art has been born."

Liadov, speaking of Scriabin[29]

"I am sitting here alone, admiring the view of the gloomy Heidelberg castle shrouded in grey haze. But even in this weather it is so captivating! No matter where you glance, everything here is a symbol of the stern but beautiful centuries gone

Scriabin's First Piano Sonata, the first of his works to be published by Belaieff.

forever!"

A. Scriabin
(from a letter to Natalia Sekerin,
Heidelberg, May 1895)[30]

In spring 1895, Scriabin made his first trip abroad.

Acquaintance (and later, friendship) with Belaieff, who supported Scriabin materially in every way, made it possible for the composer to devote his time to creative work.

Besides the high royalties, Scriabin was a recipient in 1897-1909 and in 1911 of the so-called "Glinka prize" (founded by Belaieff). Belaieff also gave to Scriabin a grand piano and the complete works of Chopin; in 1895-1896 he sponsored the composer on a rest tour and on concert engagements abroad.

"Nevertheless I must say that, no matter how beautiful Europe is, for a Russian nothing can replace a Russian village; it has a special inexplicable charm that comes from its wide, open spaces."

A. Scriabin
(from a letter to Natalia Sekerin,
Heidelberg, May 1895)[31]

In Witznau, on Lake Vierwaldstätten, Scriabin underwent treatment for his hand. There, he wrote his Preludes Op. 11, No. 12 (G sharp Minor), No. 17 (A flat Major), No. 18 (F Minor), No. 23 (F Major); the Impromptus Op. 12, No. 1 (F sharp Major), Op. 14, No. 2 (F sharp Minor); and Prelude Op. 16, No. 2 (G sharp Minor).

In 1896, Belaieff organized Scriabin's first concert tour abroad. Scriabin gave recitals in Paris, and also in Belgium, Germany, and Holland.

"Scriabin, the 24-year-old Russian composer and pianist from Moscow, gave in Erard Hall one of the most remarkable recitals that we have recently heard. We have encountered an exceptional person, a superb composer and pianist, a great individual and philosopher; he is utter passion and sacred flame. . ."

Eugène George.
Review of Scriabin's January 3/15, 1896
Paris recital in La Libre Critique
(Free Criticism)[32]

"All his works show his indisputable individuality, and in his playing he reveals that subtle and peculiar charm of the Slavs—the best pianists in the world. Scriabin: remember well this name."

Gustave Doret
(composer, conductor, and writer on music).
Review of Scriabin's concert in Paris in 1896[33]

"The concert of March 16 was a tremendous success, and the nocturne for the left hand made a great impression".

A. Scriabin
(from a letter to Belaieff,
Paris, April 1896)[34]

"I hasten to inform you about the outcome of my second recital . . .The house was full, and the success so tremendous that I

The Sonata-fantasy of which Alexander Scriabin made a gift to Natalia Sekerin. Autograph.

Scriabin in the village of Zenino, where he stayed with his Conservatory friend Emil Rosenov in 1894.

Mitrofan Belaieff (1836-1903), a wealthy timber merchant, patron of
the arts and music. Portrait by the famous Russian artist Ilya Repin.

Belaieff's letter to Scriabin concerning the publication of the Second Piano Sonata.

Left to right: Anatoly Lyadov, Alexander Glazunov, Nikolai Rimsky-Korsakov.

wish I ever had one like it in Russia."

A. Scriabin
(from a letter to Belaieff,
Paris, April 1896)[35]

The first Glinka prize of 1000 rubles was presented to Scriabin in 1897 for his Mazurkas Op. 3, Allegro Op. 4, Sonata Op. 6, Impromptus Op. 7, Prelude and Nocturne Op. 9. Later, Scriabin would receive the Glinka prize almost every year for piano and symphonic works, among them his poem *Prometheus* in 1911.

Scriabin's works immediately entered repertoires of other pianists.

"I met Lamoureux, at whose house Levin played Rubinstein's concerto, as well as three of my etudes, very well indeed. I received a letter from a Dutch pianist who asked if he could appear in a recital of my compositions at your concert."

A. Scriabin
(from a letter to Belaieff,
Paris, 1896)[36]

(Charles Lamoureux, 1834-1899, was the conductor who in the 1880-1890s founded and headed the regular Concerts Lamoureux.)

". . .He [A. Scriabin—ed.] played for the entire evening, and, they say, played better than he had in a long time. . .He won the hearts of both Hoffmanns, father and son, and the latter the very next day began to practice two of his mazurkas and two etudes, subsequently to play them in St. Petersburg in a concert."

L.A. Scriabin
(from a letter to Belaieff,
January, 1897)[37]

"Goldenweiser played. It was a prelude by Scriabin. Lev Nikolayevich liked it very much.

" 'Very sincere, and sincerity is a rare thing,' he said. 'This one piece is proof that he is a great artist.' "

V. Bulgakov[38]

Witznau.

". . .At the time I did not play much Scriabin; for him [for Tolstoy—ed.] I played only several preludes, the Etude Op. 2, in C sharp Minor, and the Mazurka in F sharp Major, which he liked so much that he always asked me to play it again. When in 1904 we lived at a dacha near 'Kosaya Gora,' Lev Nikolayevich [Tolstoy] once rode up to our house. My wife was playing the first movement of Scriabin's second Sonata (the Sonata-fantasy). Lev Nikolayevich stood listening for quite a long time and then asked me what she had been playing, and said that he liked it very much."

A. Goldenweiser[39]

". . .I love the sea so much and always yearn for it."

A. Scriabin
(from a letter to Natalia Sekerin,
Heidelberg, 1895)[40]

"The Second Sonata (Sonata-fantasy) was started in 1892 and published only in 1897. Scriabin used to say that it was inspired by the sea. The first movement is a quiet, southern night on the seashore. In the development, a dark, stormy deep sea. The E-major part is the tender moonlight that comes after the dark. The second movement (Presto) is an image of the wide, turbulent expanse of the sea."

J. Engel[41]

The first movement of the Second sonata was written in 1896, the second movement was composed in early 1890s, and the sonata as a whole was completed in 1897.

Scriabin made his first journey by sea in 1892 (from St. Petersburg to Riga); in the summer of 1893 he lived in Gurzuf, and in the summer of 1895 in Genoa).

In 1897, Scriabin married Vera Isakovich, who would become an acclaimed performer of Scriabin's music, her repertoire featuring his first sonatas, small pieces, and the piano part of *Prometheus*.

"A young brilliant pianist, she graduated from the Schlözer class of the Moscow conservatory (with a gold medal) only in the spring of the same year [1897 – Ed.]. . .

"They met on December 6, 1893, at a student party in memory of Nikolai Rubinstein, where Vera happened to play. When introduced to Vera, Scriabin said: 'When you played I thought: here, at last is a woman pianist I can listen to with pleasure.' "

J. Engel[42]

(Pavel Schlözer (1848-1898), a pupil of Liszt, was a professor at the Moscow conservatory from 1891 to 1898.)

"*My student* Scriabin has written a *marvellous* piano concerto. Since this young man is on the road to fame—he has played with enormous success in Paris, Amsterdam, Brussels, and Berlin; and is going on tour again this fall—I would like to take advantage of his staying with us and include him in the program. . . Amateurs and the public will hear a premiere which is certain to make a sensation in the musical world, and Odessa will have the honor of the initiative."

V. Safonov
(from a letter to the Odessa branch
of the Russian Music Society, 1897)[43]

"Yesterday, the Odessa tour was over. Scriabin's recital of his marvellous Concerto was a great success".

V. Safonov
(from a letter to Cui, 1897)[44]

"The Third Sonata is the climactic point in the development of the first stage of Scriabin's artistic career. It is a brilliant summing up of the entire period."

E. Gunst[45]

Scriabin included the following program with the Third Sonata (his authorship of the program is not documented; the program, or commentary, was written by his second wife Tatiana Schloezer, and authorized by Scriabin):

1st movement: "A free and wild soul rushes passionately into the abyss of suffering and struggle."

2nd movement: "The soul has found an imaginary, immediate,

Pianist and composer Alexander Goldenweiser (author of the two-volume reminiscences *Near Tolstoy*) playing in Yasnaya Polyana, Tolstoy's residence. Goldenweiser (1875-1961) was also a professor at the Moscow Conservatory.

Vera Isakovich (1875-1920) in 1897.

Rimsky-Korsakov (1844-1908).

and delusive repose; worn out by suffering, it seeks oblivion, it wants to sing and bloom. . . But the light rhythm and fragrant harmonies are only a veil over the restless and hurt soul. . ."

3rd movement: "The soul has surrendered to the flow in a sea of feeling, tender and sad: love, wistfulness, vague desires, inexplicable thoughts, the spell of a delicate dream. . . Seeking oblivion. . ."

4th movement: "In the storm of the liberated elements, the soul is struggling in the ecstasy of battle; the awesome voice of Man, the Creator, rises from the abyss of Being, and his victorious song resounds triumphantly. But, too weak to reach the summit, he tumbles, temporarily defeated, into the abyss of Nothingness."[46]

From 1898 to 1903, Scriabin was a professor of the piano class at the Moscow Conservatory. Teaching was a burden to him, but he established a reputation as a remarkable pedagog.

"All his remarks were very concise: 'One must extract sound from a wooden instrument like precious ore from the dry earth. . .' Scriabin's instructions concerning the pedal, of which he was a virtuoso master, were exceptionally interesting. . . Alexander had his own special types of pedal: the 'vibrating,' the 'pin pedal,' the 'pedal mist.'"

M. Nemenov-Lunz[47]

"At the time, the illustrious Alexander Scriabin was professor of the piano class at the Conservatory. . . Since he was also professor of the piano at the Yekaterinin Institute. . . and used to arrange concerts for the students of the Institute there, Alexander often invited me to participate. . .

"At the concert, where all the students and the staff were present, Alexander played his works beautifully, and then accompanied me."

Antonina Nezhdanov[48]

"It is the most terrible time for me: exams at the Institute, 12 evenings in a row (350 students), a lot of lessons at the Conservatory too, in short—music from 2 to midnight. But I keep composing at night: as luck would have it, many good ideas come to me in spring."

*Scriabin
(from a letter to Belaieff,
March 1902)*[49]

In 1903 Scriabin gave up his teaching career so that he could devote all his time to creative work.

In 1898, Scriabin wrote the orchestral miniature *Dreams* - the first symphonic work he completed.

"Today I attended the rehearsal of the prelude, and, fancy my joy, it sounds quite good indeed. Rimsky-Korsakov was so kind, listened to all the instruments separately, rehearsed with them

The Second Sonata. The cover of the Belaieff edition.

for a whole hour."

A. Scriabin
(from a letter to his wife Vera Scriabin,
St. Petersburg, December 1898)[50]

The first performance of the symphonic poem (or prelude, as Scriabin called it) was in St. Petersburg on December 5, 1898, with Rimsky-Korsakov conducting. In Moscow, *Dreams* was performed on March 18, 1899, with Safonov on the podium.

In 1900 Scriabin completed the First Symphony (Op. 26, E Major) for orchestra, chorus, and soloists. He also wrote the entire text for the finale.

"I cannot adequately express my admiration for your new symphony. . . I am looking forward to obtaining the proof copy of the score so I can prepare your marvellous work for a concert in the fall."

V. Safonov
(from a letter to Scriabin,
June 1900)[51]

"Come, all the peoples of the world,
Let us sing in praise of Art."

Scriabin's text for the finale
of the first symphony

Once he finished his first Symphony, Scriabin unveiled it to the Belaieff circle.

"I have already played it for Liadov. He is coming again today, and we shall prepare it so it can be played by others on two pianos."

A. Scriabin
(from a letter to his wife V. Scriabin,
January 1900)[52]

Scriabin's first Symphony was first performed on November 11, 1900 in St. Petersburg, under the direction of Liadov.

". . . Liadov was a truly gifted conductor . . . strong, nervous and delicate, and Scriabin's symphonies acquired in his loving, caring, and nobly exalted interpretation both graphic elegance of form and expressive vitality."

A. Ossovsky[53]

"The symphony has made a good, heart-warming and very nice impression. . . The symphony consists of six parts; the last one was not performed because it is written with chorus."

From a review of the concert of
November 11, 1900[54]

In Moscow, the First Symphony was first performed with a chorus on March 16, 1901 in the Hall of Columns of the Nobles' Assembly, with Safonov conducting, in a concert of the Moscow Chapter of the Russian Music Society. It featured the singers

The finale of Scriabin's First Symphony. A page of the score.

73

Alexander Scriabin in 1901.

СИМФОНИЧЕСКІЕ КОНЦЕРТЫ

2.

программа.

ЗАЛЪ ДВОРЯНСКАГО СОБРАНІЯ

Въ Субботу, 11-го Ноября,

ВТОРОЙ

РУССКІЙ СИМФОНИЧЕСКІЙ КОНЦЕРТЪ

ПОДЪ УПРАВЛЕНІЕМЪ

Ан. К. ЛЯДОВА.

The program of the second of the Russian Symphonic Concerts conducted by Lyadov, in which Scriabin's First Symphony was premiered.

Petrova and Shubin, and the combined choirs of the Moscow Conservatory and the Russian Choral Society.

"Many thanks to Vassily Ilyich! How beautifully he did the First in Moscow!" (A. Scriabin).

"The originality of Mr. Scriabin is genuine: he has his own artistic individuality, manner, and style, of which the specific characteristics become apparent at a closer look. And his works, despite their complexity, are quite sincere: the composer wrote them 'without respect of persons,' knowing no other judge than his own artistic conscience, regardless of the requirements of the public, requiring of it instead new and very high standards."

> *S. Trubetzkoy*
> *(from the article "On Scriabin's concert,"*
> *in* The Courier, *No. 63, 1902)*[55]

Trubetzkoy was editor of the magazine *Philosophical and Psychological Issues* and author of several philosophical works of an idealistic orientation. Contacts with Trubetzkoy helped Scriabin to develop his philosophical views (on Trubetzkoy's invitation he attended meetings of the Moscow Philosophical Society). (For details see J. Engel, "A.N. Scriabin," *Musical Contemporary,* No. 4/5, 1916).

Scriabin's Second Symphony was first performed in St. Petersburg on January 12, 1902, with Liadov conducting.

"... In his music one detects the aroma of life, tense and impetuous, fresh, inquisitively eager to get a glimpse of the future but never helpless melancholy, never renunciation of struggle."

> *J. Engel*[56]

The premiere of the Second Symphony (in St. Petersburg and particularly in Moscow) evoked ambivalent public reaction; reviewers pointed out a certain questioning, uneven quality alongside its merits.

"... After the performance of the symphony was over, half of the audience made their way to the stage with roaring applause. The other half remained in their seats. There was a terrible clamor, hissing, whistling... The more one group hissed, the more the other group applauded. An unbelievable noise rocked the house. The applause was so strong that Alexander had to come out on the stage, and so did Safonov. Pale, but absolutely calm, even smiling Alexander Nikolaevich was looking at his audience."

> *L.A. Scriabin*
> *(from her reminiscences about the first*
> *performance of the Second Symphony in Moscow)*[57]

Antonina Nezhdanov (1873-1950), a student at the Moscow Conservatory from 1899 to 1902.

1903-1908
Artistic Prime

The most productive years of Scriabin's creative work were a time of great social upheaval at the beginning of the century.

"Storm, soon a storm will burst!"

A. Gorky[58]

"I shall go to tell people that they are strong and powerful!"
A. Scriabin[59]

". . . The music of the Third Symphony is . . . comprehended as the powerful self-assertion of a Man, as an artistic image of the highest optimism."

A. Alschwang[60]

"In the spring of 1903, my father rented a dacha in Obolenskoye, near Maloyaroslavets. . . Scriabin happened to be our neighbor. . .

"As usual, we arrived at the dacha early in the morning. . . I ran out into the forest.

"My God, it was brimming with everything that morning! It was pierced by the sun all directions. . . And just as sun and shade alternated in the wood and birds sang and flew from one branch to another, bits and pieces from the Third Symphony, or the *Divine poem* which was being composed in the piano version at the next dacha, were flying and rolling in the air.

"Oh God, what a music it was! The symphony was crashing and collapsing again and again, like a town under artillery fire, and then it built up and grew out of the wreckage and ruins. It was brimming with an essence chiseled out to the point of insanity, and as new as the forest was new, full of life and breathing freshness. . ."

Boris Pasternak[61]

"Yesterday night, I finally played my symphony for the crowd of St. Petersburg composers, and what a surprise! Glazunov was delighted and Rimsky-Korsakov was also very favorable. At dinner we even discussed how nice it would be if we got Nikisch to perform it."

A. Scriabin
(from a letter to Vera Scriabin,
St. Petersburg, November 1903)[62]

Dreams. Cover of the score (the Belaieff edition).

Alexander Glazunov (1865-1936).

1902.

ВЪ БОЛЬШОМЪ ЗАЛѢ

МОСКОВСКОЙ КОНСЕРВАТОРІИ

во *Вторникъ, 5-го Марта,*

КОНЦЕРТЪ

А. Н. СКРЯБИНА

съ уч. оркестра и хора, подъ упр. **В. И. Сафонова.**

ПРОГРАММА.

1. А. Н. Скрябинъ: Симфонія для оркестра, голосовъ соло и хора, E-dur. соч. 26.

 а) Lento.
 б) Allegro dramatico.
 в) Lento.
 г) Vivace.
 д) Allegro.
 е) Andante.

The program of the first performance of Scriabin's First Symphony in Moscow, under the baton of Vasily Safonov. The program includes the text of the poem Scriabin wrote to accompany the music:

 Great image of the Deity,
 Of harmonies the lofty art!
 United all, we bring to thee
 Delighted praises from the heart.

 Thou art the shining dream of life,
 Thou art a feast, thou art a rest,
 Thy wondrous visions are a gift
 By which humanity is blessed.

 In those dark hours when grim despair
 Our spirit threatens to destroy,
 It is in thee that beings find
 A comfort and a living joy.

Alexander Scriabin in 1903.

Sergei Trubetzkoy (1862-1905), professor of philosophy and the first
elected president of the University of Moscow; Scriabin's friend and
enthusiastic admirer of his work.

At the same time as the Third Symphony, Scriabin wrote the Fourth Sonata. In the commentaries, the composer made his first allusion to the connection between his musical and light-color images: the blue dream-star is lit up by the music of the sun. It was in the Fourth Sonata that the symbolic and philosophical type of the Scriabin program was first outlined. "The Fourth Sonata," the composer wrote in one of his letters, "has an unpublished text, written after the music was composed."

"I am drinking you, O sea of light! I, the light, engulf you!"

A. Scriabin
(from the text to the
Fourth Sonata)[63]

"I want it *even faster,* as fast as possible, on the *verge of the possible* . . . it must be a flight at the speed of light, right towards the sun, into the sun!"

A. Scriabin
(performing directions
for the Fourth Sonata Presto)[64]

"I am working on piano pieces, among which there is an etude excelling the Third Symphony in power and sublimity."

A. Scriabin
(from a letter to B. Schloezer,
August 1903)[65]

"I played your Fourth sonata a great deal and admired it a great deal as well. Will you put it on the program, or one of the other sonatas? I would prefer the Fourth, which is original, full of ravishing beauty, and the thoughts in it are expressed with extreme clarity and conciseness."

A. Glazunov
(from a letter to A. Scriabin,
February 1905)[66]

In spring 1904, the Scriabin family left for Switzerland.
"I preferred to live abroad because life in Russia, especially in Moscow, with our inability to organize our time, was hardly conducive to the discipline necessary to accomplish my task."

A. Scriabin
(from a letter to N. Findeisen,
December 1907)[67]

"We have a pretty little house. . . Sasha has a room on top with a piano (there is not a single grand piano in all of Geneva), and he can seclude himself there."

Vera Scriabin
(from a letter to
Z. Monighetti,
March 1904)[68]

A page of the Third Symphony score. Autograph.

"Switzerland in winter is not any worse than in summer. Such a delicate play of the most tender colors. The outline of the mountains is almost imperceptible, everything is in a blue haze. Everything is a hint, everything a promise and a dream."

A. Scriabin
(from a letter to
Tatiana Schloezer,
January 1905)[69]

Scriabin had an enduring interest in philosophy. In 1904 he attended the sessions of the Second International Philosophical Congress in Geneva. The published collection of records of the Second International Philosophical Congress sessions includes a list of participants, on which Scriabin's name appears. Scriabin made numerous notes in his copy of the collection, which is now in his private library in the Scriabin Museum.

Scriabin and his wife broke up in 1905. An important reason for their separation was her lack of sympathy with his philosophical aspirations and with his dream of transforming the world through his art.

On her return to Russia in September 1905 after her break with Alexander, Vera Scriabin became a teacher at the Moscow Conservatory and then professor at the St. Petersburg Conservatory. She performed in concert extensively, popularizing Scriabin's music, and was the first pianist to devote her recitals exclusively to Scriabin's music.

A winter landscape in Switzerland.

"The novelty of the evening was Scriabin's Third Symphony, Op. 43 in C Major. . . . Scriabin is a composer who has much to say about his ideas, his theory of life and philosophy; he provides audacious, free, and massive orchestral combinations; he is gifted, young, and full of enthusiasm; his music is extremely interesting and original. Arthur Nikisch, who conducted with remarkable lucidity and precision, greatly contributed to the success of the performance of the new Scriabin work."

From The Musical Courier, *No. 26, 1905*[70]

The Third Symphony was first performed in St. Petersburg on March 8, 1906, with Blumenfeld conducting.

"In this symphony, one sees how much you have *grown!* Now you are a musician of stature. *Nobody here has ever written* a work of the same kind, quality, form, or content as your symphony!"

V. Stasov
(from a letter to Scriabin,
February 28, 1906)[71]

In June 1905, Scriabin settled with his second wife Tatiana Schloezer in the Italian town of Bogliasco.

"We met Alexander Scriabin and his wife Tatiana in February 1906 on the Riviera in the small town of Bogliasco. . . .

"It appeared that Alexander Nikolaevich, who had long been away from Russia and was fully absorbed in his new musical

Etude № 5.

Etude in C-sharp minor Op. 42. First page of the edition. This piece,
Scriabin believed, "excelled the Third Symphony in power and sublimity."

The house in the Vesenaz settlement on Lake Geneva, where Scriabin
lived with his family and finished his Third Symphony.

Vera Scriabin.

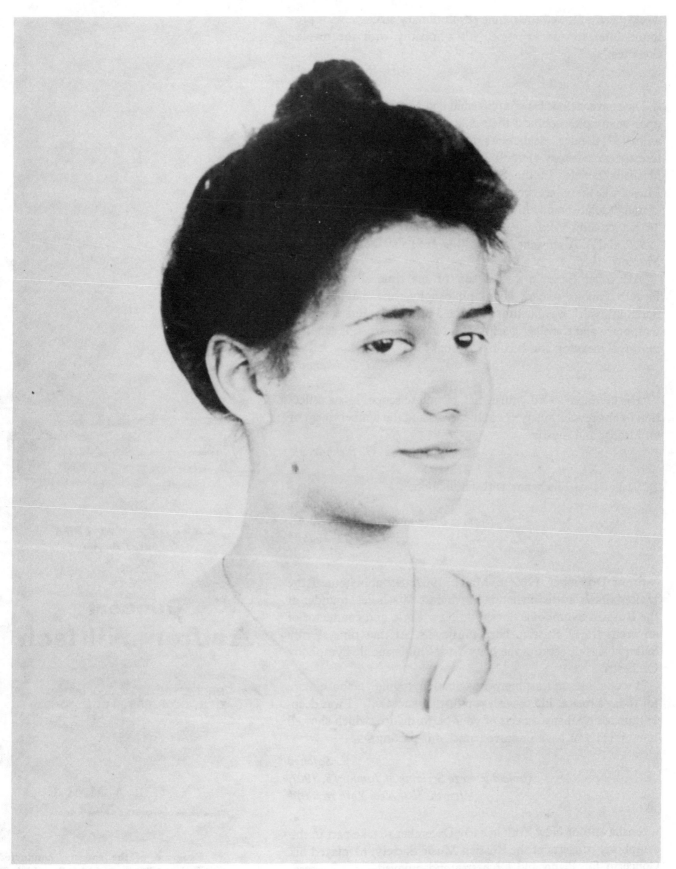

Tatiana Schloezer (1883-1922), Scriabin's second wife.

works, also followed the heroic revolutionary struggle with profound interest, and expressed his sympathy with the revolutionaries."

Mrs. R. Plekhanov[72]

The conversations between Scriabin and Mr. Plekhanov touched upon many philosophical themes, and their disputes were quite animated. Under Plekhanov's influence, Scriabin became interested in Marxist literature, although it did not change his idealistic beliefs. In the Scriabin library (the Scriabin State Museum), there are books Plekhanov gave him as presents (among them, some of his own works). (For details, see J. Engel, "A.N. Scriabin," *Musical Contemporary, Alexander Scriabin: 1915 - 1940,* and A. Alschwang, *Selected Works in Two Volumes,* vol. 2, Moscow, 1965.)

"Alexander Scriabin was a son of his time. Paraphrasing Hegel's famous remark about philosophy, one may say that Scriabin's work was his time expressed in sounds. But when the temporary and transient is expressed by a great artist, it acquires *universal* meaning and becomes eternal."

G. Plekhanov[73]

"His [Scriabin's - Ed.] music has grandiose scope. It is a reflection of our revolutionary era in the views and the temperament of an idealist and mystic."

G. Plekhanov[74]

"Sasha reads Plekhanov with fascination."

T. Schloezer
(from a letter to M. Nemenov-Lunz,
February 20, 1905)[75]

From December 1906 to March 1907, Scriabin toured the United States at the invitation of Modest Altschuler, founder of the Russian Symphonic Society in New York, and conductor of an orchestra of Russian-born musicians. At that time, Vasily Safonov was director of the New York Philharmonic Symphony Orchestra.

"I would like, at least in my imagination, to hug you once more for today's recital and to wish you further success. . . I was deeply touched by many aspects of your performance, which showed how much you have improved since our parting."

V. Safonov
(from a letter to Scriabin of January 3, 1907,
after the first New York recital)[76]

"Sasha left for New York in early December to take part in the symphony concerts of the Russian Music Society; he played his Concerto for Piano and Orchestra and enjoyed great success; then he gave two recitals in New York, then played in Chicago, Detroit, and Cincinnati—everywhere with tremendous success.

Program of the concert, conducted by Arthur Nikisch, in which Scriabin's Third Symphony was premiered.

"... I had the pleasure of hearing the first Symphony, brilliantly conducted by Modest Altschuler; the public liked the symphony very much. The Third Symphony, performed two weeks later, also by Altschuler, in the final concert of the season, was received enthusiastically both by the public and by musicians."

T. Schloezer
(from a letter to M. Nemenov-Lunz,
Paris, April 1907)[77]

Scriabin's Third Symphony was also conducted by Altschuler in concerts of the Russian Symphonic Society.

"I want to create freely. To create consciously."

A. Scriabin[78]

"... Soon midnight will come. Everybody is asleep. I am sitting alone in the dining-room and composing, or rather, thinking over for the thousandth time the plan for my new work."

A. Scriabin
(from a letter to T. Schloezer,
Vésenaz, January 1905)[79]

"... Here [in Switzerland - Ed.] Maria Lunz and her husband are for the summer, and this, of course, makes our life much more pleasant. Maria never misses a chance to go through all of my last works with me, to be able to present them in Moscow as they really are. My last compositions are so complicated in mood that I am happy to be in a position to give some personal instructions about their performance to a musician who is both talented and devoted to my art."

A. Scriabin
(from a letter to M. Morozov,
Beatenberg, August 1907).[80]

"Scriabin had inner strength, integrity and conviction... Frail as he was at first glance, Alexander Nikolaevich was extremely hard-working, and his fortitude was remarkable. In him, titanic ideas were combined with a simple, childlike, serene ingenuousness, an open and trusting soul, and a rare charm that won him the hearts of people of 'different sorts.'"

Maria Nemenov-Lunz[81]

"The radiant poem (*The Poem of Ecstasy*) was composed in a tiny half-dark garret rented from the owner of a greengrocer's [in Bogliasco - Ed.]. There was a jolly din and hum of voices in the store from early morning until late into the night . . . for composing he had a broken piano, which was one and a half tones lower than normal pitch and was rented from a café. Trains roared past the windows. Despite all this, despite constant worries about making ends meet, Alexander never uttered a word of complaint . . . he was working on his new composition in ecstasy, with feverish enthusiasm."

Maria Nemenov-Lunz[82]

The program of Scriabin's benefit recital in Geneva for the families of Russian political emigres, organized by Mrs. Plekhanov, on June 30, 1906.

A view of Bogliasco. Scriabin is seen in the background, with his back to the camera.

Pianist Maria Nemenov-Lunz (1879-1954), a student and friend of Scriabin.

Modest Altschuler (1873-1963) and Vassily Safonov (1852-1918) in the
United States.

Felix Blumenfeld, well-known orchestra and opera conductor, professor of piano at the St. Petersburg, Kiev, and Moscow Conservatories, and the first to perform *The Poem of Ecstasy* in St. Petersburg.

"Tonight Sasha is playing and reciting *The Poem of Ecstasy*. We have invited the Korsakov family, Blumenfeld, Rachmaninoff and Margarita Morozov."

T. Schloezer[83]

For the *Poem of Ecstasy*, Scriabin wrote a literary program in verse, in the spirit of Symbolist poetry. Apparently realizing the considerable discrepancy between the text and the music, the composer decided against publishing it along with the score, and had it published separately. The music of *The Poem of Ecstasy* made a strong impression on those who attended the composer's first presentation of it; the text read by Scriabin was not received very well. (See Miss N. Rimsky-Korsakov, "N. Rimsky-Korsakov and A. Scriabin," *Soviet Music*, No 5, 1950 and "Rimsky-Korsakov," V. Yastrebtzev's *Reminiscences*, vol. 2, Leningrad, 1960, pp. 423-424.)

In Lausanne, Scriabin finished *Poem of Ecstasy* and wrote his Fifth Piano Sonata. There, he met conductor Sergei Koussevitzky, who later became a performer and publisher of his music after founding an impresario and publishing business: regular series of symphony concerts and the Russian Music Publishing House. Koussevitzky published Scriabin's works in 1909-1911.

In August 1908, Scriabin and his wife stayed in Biarritz at Koussevitzky's. It was there that Sudbinin, a pupil of Rodin, did a bust of the composer.

"Today I have just about completed the Fifth Sonata—a big poem for piano—and consider it my best piano work.

A. Scriabin
(from a letter to M. Morozov,
Lausanne, November 1907)[84]

Striving for a more concentrated realization of his ideas, Scriabin arrived at one-movement forms. Beginning with the Fifth, all his sonatas are in one movement.

In January 1909, Scriabin came to Russia to participate in the concerts where the *Poem of Ecstasy* was first performed. After his two-month tour, he returned abroad.

"The hero of the concert was Scriabin, composer, who is not yet 40 but whose already well-known name ignites the most fervent controversies: for some, his music is utter nonsense, for others it is a revelation of genius... After the performance of *The Poem of Ecstasy* under the baton of Blumenfeld, the composer was wildly called for, and his success was enormous."

V. Valter
(from a review of the
January 31, 1909 concert in St. Petersburg)[85]

"Scriabin's arrival in Moscow, after five years away from it, was a very happy event for his admirers. The papers had announced his arrival and his concerts. Both the symphony and the chamber concerts were a great success, the house was packed,

Margarita Morozov (1873-1958), a student and friend of Scriabin's who, for several years, gave him financial assistance. Extracts from her reminiscences of Scriabin were published in the *Soviet Music* magazine (no. 1, 1972); the manuscript is in the Scriabin State Museum.

and there was an atmosphere of celebration. The public gave Scriabin an emotional welcome. He was surrounded by an eager crowd of young people. *The Poem of Ecstasy* and *The Divine Poem* (the Third Symphony) were performed under the baton of Cooper with a very enlarged orchestra; for *The Poem of Ecstasy,* even big bells had been brought, which sounded very beautifully in the finale and made it even more magnificent and extraordinary."

Margarita Morozov[86]

The first page of Scriabin's letter to Felix Blumenfeld. "Dear Felix Mikhailovich, accept my sincere and profound gratitude for the marvellous performance of my [Third] Symphony, of which I have learned from many newspapers and also from the letters of several friends. What you have done is a miracle. . ."

Conductor Alexander Chessin (1869-1955), a pupil of Arthur Nikisch.
He was the first to perform *The Poem of Ecstasy* in Germany.

Sergei Koussevitzky (1874-1951), conductor and contrabass player, a
longtime collaborator of Scriabin.

Alexander Scriabin in Brussels, in 1909.

1909-1915
The Final Years of Life and Work
Concert Career

"Prometheus is the noblest saint and martyr in the philosophical calendar."

Karl Marx[87]

"Prometheus is a symbol that appears in different forms in all ancient teachings. It represents the active energy of the universe, the creative principle; it is fire, light, life, striving, effort, and thought."

Alexander Scriabin[88]

"The greatest men of arts—from the tragedian Aeschylus to Goethe, from Beethoven to Scriabin—all recreated the noble image of the hero of the ancient Greek myth. The characterization Scriabin gives it is a most universal one: Prometheus is 'the creative principle,' the proud, all-conquering human will, victorious over everything that had opressed it, tortured it, tried to destroy it; it is the joyous spirit of fire, symbol of the invincible power of Man."

A. Alschwang[89]

Beethoven wrote music for the ballet *The Creatures of Prometheus* (1800-1801); one of its themes was also used by the composer in his Piano Variations, Op. 35, and in the finale of the Third Symphony (*Eroica*).

Liszt's symphonic poem *Prometheus* and Taneyev's chorus of the same name (from his cycle *Twelve choruses*, Op. 27) were also dedicated to the Prometheus theme.

"This Sunday we shall have a small gathering: Professor Sigogne will recite and comment on Aeschylus' *Prometheus.*"

Tatiana Schloezer
(from a letter to Maria Nemenov-Lunz,
Brussels, October 1909)[90]

A performance of Scriabin's *Prometheus*. Painting by Leonid Pasternak.

(Emile Sigogne was a professor of eloquence and rhetoric in Brussels.)

PROGRAMME

PART I

Fantasie—"The Sea" . . . . Glazuno
Dedicated to Richard Wagner (first time)

Scherzino from "Symphonietta" . . . . Ippolitow-Ivano
(MS First Time)

Letter Scene from the Opera—"Eugene Oniegin" . . . . Tschaikowsk
Miss Louise Cox and Orchestra

Fantasie—"Night on the Bald Mount" . . . . Musorgsk

PART II.
THE WORLD PREMIERE
— of —

SCRIABINE'S

POEM OF FIRE
"PROMETHEUS"

The Most Talked of Musical Composition of the Twentieth Century introducing

The New **TASTIERA PER LUCE** (Colored light Key-Board)

This will be the *first time anywhere in the world* Scriabine's work will be given a hearin
ompletely embodying the composers wishes.

The arrangements for producing the color effects have been developed with the kind o
peration of the *Electrical Testing Laboratories.*

By numerous requests it will be repeated after a short intermission in order to give those
he audience an opportunity better to acquaint themselves with the intricate score of "Prometheus

Miss Margaret Volavy will play the Solo Piano Part and Mr. Harry Rowe Shelley will be at the Organ

STEINWAY PIANO USED

Seats, $2.00 to 25 cents. Boxes $20.00 and $15.0(

Program of the *Prometheus* premiere in New York, with Altschuler
conducting.

Scriabin at the moment of completing *Prometheus*. Amateur photo by his friend A.E. Mozer (1910).

"Alexander Scriabin came to Brussels several years after his works were heard in concert at the Érard Hall. . . He was composing *Prometheus* at the time, and I will always remember the admiration I felt listening to the fragments he played as they came forth. The novelty of the harmonic language made us ecstatic; no other composer was so daringly innovative while at the same time preserving genuine syntax of writing."

Émile Bosquet,
Belgian pianist and admirer of Scriabin[91]

The symphonic poem *Prometheus (Poem of Fire)* was written for enlarged orchestra (with organ), piano and chorus (without words). The score also included a color keyboard. In St. Petersburg, *Prometheus* was first performed on March 9, 1911 under the baton of Koussevitzky, with Scriabin at the piano.

". . . Sir Henry Wood, the *Times* music critic and other people came up with the idea of performing this composition [the poem *Prometheus* - Ed.] twice on the same program. That was unheard of in England. . . After the first time through, fortunately, the audience reacted. Several whistles (practically unheard of here), immediately followed by a burst of applause—very sincere and spontaneous. The second time around, everything was much *better* than the first. The atmosphere was very open and animated. The orchestra was in excellent spirits also. The impression was really great and beautiful. After the performance, people applauded fervently and enthusiastically. Wood had to come out three times (quite extraordinary, after a new work). It might be interesting for you to know that at both performances I spotted Mr. Bernard Shaw, who was one of the most enthusiastic and applauded with all his might, and artist John Sargent, who shouted loudly: 'We want to hear it a third time!!' "

R. Newmarch
(from a letter to A. Scriabin of February 3, 1913,
about the London debut of Prometheus)[92]

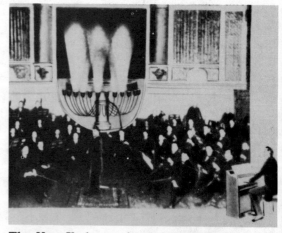

The New York premiere of *Prometheus* (with light and color effects) under the baton of Altschuler at Carnegie Hall, on March 20, 1915.

On November 9, 1913, Ziloti followed Wood's example and performed *Prometheus* twice in the same concert.

". . . Your *Prometheus* appeals to me *awfully*! It is a *colossal* work, just what I expected from you. . . *Prometheus* is such a beautiful poem that it makes me dizzy. . . As a great work should be, it is clear and simple, but requires a good, that is, a sensitive, performance. . ."

A. Ziloti
(from a letter to Scriabin
of June 7, 1911)[93]

Scriabin and Ziloti became friends after the disintegration, in 1911, of Scriabin's personal and business ties with Koussevitzky, who, nevertheless continued to perform his music. Ziloti invited Scriabin to appear in his concerts and helped arrange the publication of his works at the Jurgenson Publishing House on lucrative conditions (Jurgenson was Scriabin's last publisher during his lifetime).

The first performance of *Prometheus* with a light-color keyboard took place in Carnegie Hall, under the direction of Modest Altschuler, on March 20, 1915.

"It was absolutely inconceivable and impossible to play like Scriabin. He was a unique pianist; it was not the usual piano playing one can imitate, i.e., extract the same sounds, timbres, power, and tenderness, etc. Of course, Scriabin had all of that, but it was, so to say, of second importance in his playing. Of first importance was his special attitude towards the instrument, and that was the inimitable mystery of Scriabin alone. . .

"It is strange, but I do not remember Scriabin's physical presence on the concert stage, although I often went to his recitals. But I remember everything about his playing when he performed in our drawing-room.

". . . As soon as I heard the sounds he drew from the piano (even if my eyes were closed and I could not see his hands and fingers), I immediately felt and realized that his fingers extracted sounds not by falling on the keys, not by hitting them (which in fact they did), but in the opposite way, by pulling them from the keys and lightly soaring above them. . .

"His playing reflected his own inspired lightness, so characteristic of him, so manifest in whatever he did: in the way he walked, moved, gesticulated, and tossed his head when speaking. . . He always sat a bit further back from the keyboard than is customary. He would lean back and toss his head. And then one could not help feeling that his fingers were not falling on the keys but were fluttering above them."

Leonid Pasternak[94]

Scriabin at the piano. 1909 sketch by Leonid Pasternak.

"He [Scriabin - Ed.] had a magnificent sound, in terms of its softness and specific vibrato; also a light dexterity of fingers, and an exceptionally lively phrasing. He had no peers in the use of the pedal, and I agree with those who said that one had to look at his feet no less than at his hands. . ."

Konstantin Igumnov[95]

As early as January 1908, recordings were made by the Hupfeld company (on the "Welte-Mignon" and "Phonola" devices) of Scriabin playing his own works.

In 1910, the Symphony Orchestra of the Bolshoi Theatre, with Scriabin at the piano and Koussevitzky conducting, did a tour of the towns along the Volga River. It was an event of great significance in the musical life of the Russian provinces.

"In the evening, there was the second concert in Tver. The first one was a huge success. The hall was packed. We had a stop for several hours to see Uglich."

Tatiana Schloezer
(from a letter to M. Schloezer
of April 26, 1910)[96]

"Today will be the fifth concert in Nizhny Novgorod. Our successes have been enormous everywhere. At odd moments we

Alexander Ziloti (1863-1945), pianist and conductor.

Leonid Pasternak (1862-1945), a painter and friend of Scriabin, and the one who did several sketches of the composer playing the piano.

№ 9.

СЕЗОНЪ 1911-1912 ГОДА.

ИМПЕРАТОРСКОЕ

Русское Музыкальное О-во.

Новочеркасское Отдѣленіе.

Залъ Новочеркасскаго РЕАЛЬНАГО
училища.

Во Вторникъ, 10 января 1912 г.,

КОНЦЕРТЪ

піаниста-композитора

А. Н. Скрябина

The program of Scriabin's January 10, 1912 recital in Novocherkassk.

Scriabin on board the steamer *Perviy (The First)* during his Volga concert tour.

visited monasteries, historic sites, etc."

T. Schloezer
(from a letter to M. Schloezer
of May 3, 1910)[97]

During the Volga tour, Scriabin met the German artist Robert Sterl, whom Koussevitzky had invited to travel with them on the concert tour. The artist did sketches of the Volga towns, and also of a number of Scriabin's recitals.

In his last years, Scriabin made many concert tours, playing his piano works all over Russia as well as abroad.

A series of 1912 concerts, with Willem Mengelberg conducting and Scriabin at the piano, enjoyed great success in Holland (The Hague, Amsterdam, Haarlem) and in Germany, in Frankfort-on-the-Main.

In the autumn of 1913 in Lausanne, Scriabin met Stravinsky, to whom he introduced his latest works.

"Yesterday I played your Seventh Sonata and my opinion was not changed. I am looking forward to seeing you, so I can show and tell you what appeals to me the most in it!"

Igor Stravinsky
(from a letter to A. Scriabin
of September 1913)[98]

"The concert of November 14 was among the best of the season. The whole program was devoted to Scriabin. The house was overcrowded—the best evidence that he is loved and understood. The concert started with the First Symphony. . . The composer was called for, received a great ovation, and was presented with flowers. . ."

Review of the concert of November 14, 1913[99]

"He [Scriabin - Ed.] spent the summer of 1913 with his family in the Kaluga province on the Petrovskoy estate, on the very banks of the Oka River near the town of Aleksino, where, I remember, we used to go for walks. Baltrushaitis was Scriabin's nearest neighbor."

B. Schloezer[100]

Scriabin with Tatiana Schloezer and his friend and biographer Leonid Sabaneyev (left) in 1912.

The final three sonatas were completed in Petrovskoy (the last of them being the Eighth); it was there that the idea of *L'Acte préalable* was born.

"Let me congratulate you on your last works, and particularly the *Ninth Sonata,* which I consider a work of *inestimable value!*"

Feruccio Busoni
(from a letter to A. Scriabin, 1913)[101]

L'Acte préalable—an uncompleted work by Scriabin, which the composer regarded as an artistic preliminary to *The Mystery*—exists only in rough sketches. Scriabin conceived it as a grandiose improvisation, in which everyone present would also be a participant. The composer wanted to accomplish this in synthetic art forms.

"It is a forest!. . . It is the sounds and moods of the forest. . . This sonata will be absolutely different. . . It will be joyously radiant and earthy. . ."

A. Scriabin on the Tenth Sonata[102]

Scriabin's London recitals in the spring of 1914 were a stunning success. He not only received public acclaim and understanding, but also met many interesting and outstanding people.

On his London engagement, he was accompanied by A.N. Brianchaninov (1874 - 1918?), editor of the magazine *New Link*, who sympathized with Scriabin's philosophical interests. (Later, as chairman of the Scriabin society, which existed in the first years after the composer's death, he advocated a theosophical interpretation of Scriabin's music.)

In London, Scriabin met music critic Rosa Newmarch and Charles Myers, professor of psychology at the Universtiy of Cambridge, who was working on the subject of light-color perception, and in this connection was very much interested in Scriabin's work and his ideas of sound-color art.

". . . Tomorrow A[lexander] N[ikolaevich Brianchaninov - Ed.] and I leave for Cambridge for a whole day. We were invited there by two professors who had become interested in the light-symphony and my idea in general. I am looking forward to an interesting conversation."

A. Scriabin
(from a letter to T. Schloezer
of March 24, 1914)[103]

"He had his *favorite* compositions which he played almost every time and went back to them over and over. Among them, by the way, were the Poem Op. 32 (the First), which he played with amazing sound, Prelude No. 5 from Op. 11, Étude in D sharp Minor, the Twelfth (G-sharp Minor) Prelude (the last of Op. 39), *Désir*, Op. 57, *Enigma, Masque*, and some others."

L. Sabaneyev[104]

Alexander Scriabin at the piano (an amateur photograph).

In connection with his ideas for *The Mystery* and with the question of synthetic art, Scriabin was extremely interested in Moscow's artistic life. At that time he made several acquaintances among theatre personalities such as Stanislavsky, Tairov, Kachalov, Koonen, and Duncan.

"At a party given by Stanislavsky in honour of Sir Beerbohm Tree and Isadora Duncan, composer A.N. Scriabin was also present.

"Miss Duncan happened to be a great fan of our composer and told him that she would like to dance *Prometheus*. We have heard that Scriabin took a lively interest in this idea, and also promised to write something for Miss Duncan.

"At the same party, Miss Duncan improvised several dances with Scriabin himself accompanying at the piano."

In Utro Rossii (The Morning of Russia),
January 20, 1913[105]

Igor Stravinsky (1882-1971).

Scriabin with his wife and son Julian.

Great actor and theatrical director Konstantin Stanislavsky
(1863-1938). Portrait by Kamenko (1912).

Famous innovative dancer Isadora Duncan.

On November 22, 1914 and January 27, 1915, Scriabin gave benefit recitals in Moscow for war victims. With a few changes, the same program was repeated in Petrograd on February 12 and 16.

". . . In St. Petersburg, Scriabin gave two piano recitals, which were so successful that he had to come to St. Petersburg again for an extra concert, held on April 2, 1915. It was the composer's last public appearance. The impressions of these recitals are deeply engraved in my memory: Alexander Nikolaevich played with extraordinary inspiration and *élan*."

A. Ossovsky[106]

On April 7, 1915, Scriabin fell ill. On April 14/27 he died of massive blood poisoning. Everyone was shocked by the composer's sudden death. Miaskovsky wrote in a letter: "I was stunned by Scriabin's death, even though I learned about it in the worst of times. . . Even those who realize the greatness of the phenomenon that was Scriabin can hardly comprehend the enormity of this loss. . . His death is horrible, as absurd as the war we are fighting. . ." The entire artistic community of Moscow attended Scriabin's funeral, as did many intellectuals and students.

Scriabin's untimely death evoked responses from many men of arts. Poets Briusov, Ivanov, Baltrushaitis dedicated poems to Scriabin.

In the 1915-1916 season, several Scriabin memorial concert series were organized in Moscow by Koussevitzky, and in Petrograd by Ziloti, featuring Russia's most eminent musicians, such as Rachmannoff, Goldenweiser, Borovsky, and Romanovsky.

In many Russian cities musicians paid tribute to the memory of Scriabin. Glière gave a concert of Scriabin's symphonic works in Kiev.

Three of Scriabin's seven children—Rimma, Lev, and Julian (who was a very promising composer)—died in their childhood (Julian drowned at the age of 11 in 1919). His daughter Ariadna lived in France; during World War II she was in the French Resistance and was killed by Nazis. His daughter Helena (born 1900) is a pianist who graduated from the Leningrad Conservatory after studies with L.V. Nikolaiev, and from the Moscow Conservatory, where she was a student of Konstantin Igumnov; Maria (born 1901), a theatre actress, and then an associate of the Scriabin State Museum, is now retired; Marina (born 1911), an art critic and musicologist, lives in France.

"Julian passed his piano exam brilliantly. . . I remember the tender affection in the eyes of the examination commission members—Glière, Yavorsky and Stepovoy (Akimenko)—as they looked at him. It was a moment when all those people, different as they were, seemed to be possessed by the same feeling, the same thought about Alexander Scriabin and the spark of his genius embodied in this frail creature. That time, Julian also played some of his own preludes. It seemed to me then that they were but copies of his father's later compositions, a reflection of Scriabin's works following Op. 60. . . Now, I can see in these lit-

The Ninth Piano Sonata. Autograph.

tle preludes, written in the last months of Julian's life, something that is so rare even among more experienced composers: real musical thinking, genuine logic, clear-cut intentions, and a precise realization of them; such clarity is given to the immensely talented alone."

A. Alschwang[107]

Shortly after the composer's death, the Scriabin Society was founded; its aim was to promote the works and the aesthetic and philosophical ideas of the great musician. Among other things, the Society organized lectures and evenings dedicated to Scriabin. On March 21, 1917, in the Minor Hall of the Moscow Conservatory, the poet Balmont gave a lecture on "light-sound in nature and the light-symphony of Scriabin," later published as a booklet.

". . . I came to Moscow and saw Scriabin. This meeting will always remain imprinted on my soul as vision of dazzling musicality."

Konstantin Balmont[108]

"Scriabin was a Titan of Russian music."

Fedor Chaliapin[109]

"Scriabin has left a permanent mark on the evolution of contemporary music."

A. Glazunov[110]

"Just as Dostoyevsky is not only a novelist and Blok not only a poet, so Scriabin is not only a composer, but a cause for everlasting celebration, a festival of Russian culture and the embodiment of its triumph."

Boris Pasternak[111]

КІЕВЪ 🦅 1916 г.

КІЕВСКАЯ КОНСЕРВАТОРІЯ

ИМПЕРАТОРСКАГО

Русскаго Музыкальнаго Общества.

Въ Среду, 30-го Марта,

ВЪ ЗАЛѢ КУПЕЧЕСКАГО СОБРАНІЯ

СИМФОНИЧЕСКІЙ КОНЦЕРТЪ

подъ управленіемъ Директора Консерваторіи

Р. М. Гліэра,

съ участіемъ солистовъ и оркестра учащихся Консерваторіи.

Программа посвящена произведеніямъ

А. Н. Скрябина.

1. Симфонія E-dur, op. 26.

a) Lento.
b) Allegro dramatico.
c) Lento.
d) Vivace.
e) Allegro.

Исп. оркестръ.

Антрактъ 15 минутъ.

The program of the symphony concert of Scriabin's works, conducted by Reinhold Glière, in Kiev on March 30, 1916.

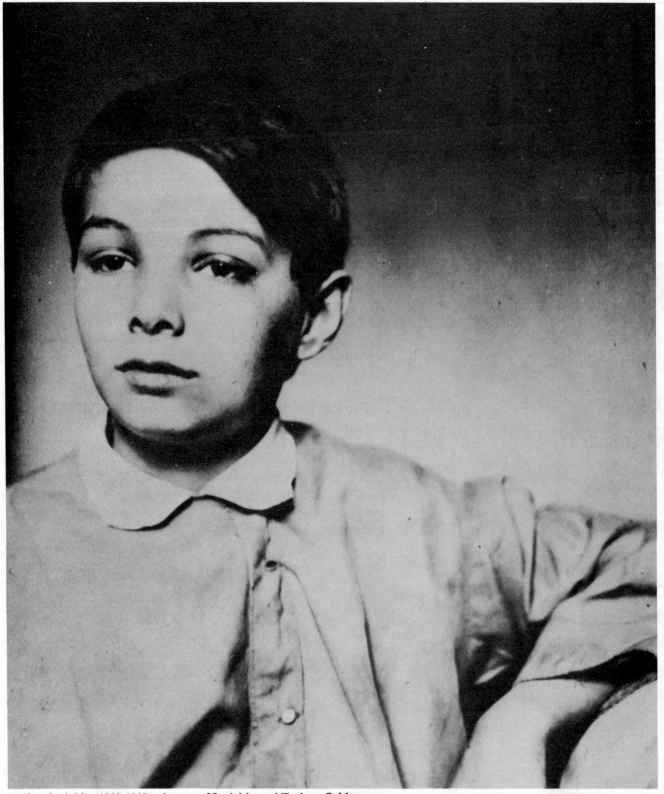

Julian Scriabin (1908-1919), the son of Scriabin and Tatiana Schloezer. He studied at the Kiev conservatory in Glière's composition class, and died in an accident (by drowning) in 1919.

Alexander Scriabin. Portrait by Golovin (1914).

Sketch of the backdrop for the performance of Scriabin's *Prometheus*.
Moscow, the Bolshoi, 1918.

Scriabin
in Soviet musical life

On November 6, 1918, in the Bolshoi theatre, a festive concert was held, dedicated to the first anniversary of the October Revolution. The program included Scriabin's *Prometheus*. Lenin attended.

"Everybody is familiar with Scriabin's theory of the spectral analogy of color and sound. This same theory gave us the idea for the background of *Prometheus*. I was commissioned to do the job. . ."

A. Lentulov[112]

"Lentulov painted the huge background for *Prometheus* with great inspiration, but music changes, whereas a colored curtain does not. Lentulov had the idea of illuminating the curtain with different colored lights according to the music, in a way that would enable the painter, although very subjectively, to paint a kind of color score of the music. The undertaking fascinated Lentulov and he scurried around the theatre and installed different filters on the lights in accordance with his score, and rehearsed his color part with the orchestra."

Mrs. M. Lentulov[113]

"The sketches for the background which I did were approved by the artistic council, which at the time included Stanislavsky and Nemirovich-Danchenko. The background recreated the spirit of the music; it was a dazzling sight, dotted with the outlines of slogans, on which the lights were switched on and off by a rheostat as the different sections of *Prometheus* began and ended. The orchestra of one hundred musicians and as many choristers all wore special costumes, in the style of medieval students' blouses and berets."

A. Lentulov[114]

"In Scriabin's music we have the highest gift of revolutionary romanticism in music. . ."

A. Lunacharsky[115]

In 1918 Scriabin's apartment was taken under the protection of the state. The order of the People's Commissariat of Education was signed by Lunacharsky, who, like Plekhanov, linked Scriabin's music with the Russian revolutionary movement of

Painter Aristarch Lentulov (1881-1943).

Rodion Shchedrin, vice chairman of the Centennial Committee, opens the Scriabin centenary meeting in the Grand Hall of the Conservatory. Moscow, January 6, 1972.

Boris Asafiev (1884-1949), academician, musicologist, composer.

Composer Nikolai Myaskovsky (1881-1950).

the early 20th century, emphasizing Scriabin's subjective reflection of the revolutionary atmosphere.

Many Soviet composers were influenced by Scriabin, especially in their formative years. Scriabin's musical influence can be felt in some of Prokofiev's early piano pieces and his orchestral composition *Dreams,* as well as, to a lesser extent, in the works of Miaskovsky (his Sixth Symphony, for example) and Shostakovich (the First Symphony), in the piano compositions of Alexandrov and Feinberg, and in the music of Krein and Gnessin.

"Scriabin enriched Russian music immensely. Piano literature is indebted to him not only because of his brilliant transmutation of the Chopin-Liszt tradition, but also because of his tremendous discoveries in the new harmonic-timbre and ornamental melodic intonations, which made it possible to portray the most intimate and delicate emotions... The composer's elevated thinking, his exceptional, refined artistic sensibility and sharp intellect . . . led to an exceedingly rapid and intense expansion of his artistic consciousness in the direction of greater and greater scope of new spheres of sound."

B. Asafiev[116]

"... What can stand comparison with this vortex of titanic force, which in its gust of enthusiasm captivates everybody—the ordinary listener, the amateur sophisticated in the latest refinements, and the tired, cynical, indifferent professional."

N. Miaskovsky on The Poem of Ecstasy[117]

"If you could only imagine how interesting Scriabin's late works are—his sonatas, *The Divine Poem, Ecstasy* . . .

S. Prokofiev
(from a letter to A. Glagolev,
July 22, 1909)[118]

"... Now we realize what a great impact Scriabin made by his quests and discoveries, what influence he had even on those composers whose development took an entirely different course. We are grateful to Scriabin for having expanded the boundaries of our art by his inexhaustible fantasy and his brilliant talent."

D. Shostakovich[119]

"Scriabin's music is dominated by a striving towards light, a proud self-consciousness devoid of all ostentation, the genuine uplift of battle, a lyricism incomparable in its purity, and a truly extraordinary drama."

A. Alschwang[120]

"In his creative individuality, Scriabin combines the greatest inspiration, emotional intensity, and ingenuousness with an extraordinary sense of purely musical beauty and proportion. His music is harmonically precise and captivatingly beautiful whether it is unassuming and simple, or violent and as if striving to escape from the bonds of reality."

A. Alexandrov[121]

The Bolshoi Theatre building.

Scriabin's music has been prominently represented in the concert programs of the most illustrious Soviet musicians.

"... *The Poem of Ecstasy*—this is how I would describe all of Scriabin's life and work. He was burning, and burning out—and that is why his music, like a star, like the sun, radiates light."

H. Neuhaus[122]

"From my childhood to my dying day my love for him will be a part of me—alive, immutable, and unshakable.

"Life, light, striving, and will—this is the true greatness of Scriabin."

V. Sofronitzky[123]

At all-Scriabin concerts, Lunacharsky would often make an introductory speech.

"... In Scriabin ... there was a powerful tendency toward the societal, the national and even the cosmic; in this he belonged to the people that went through the great revolution of 1905 and was on its way to the greatest of all revolutions."

A. Lunacharsky[124]

"Scriabin's music has such brilliant power, such truly revolutionary audacity, that its impact on a contemporary audience cannot be anything but fruitful."

A. Goldenweiser[125]

The 25th anniversary of Scriabin's death in 1940 was commemorated extensively. There were many all-Scriabin concerts; a learned session of the Soviet Composer's Union which was dedicated to him; many exhibitions, one of them at the Moscow Conservatory, and a travelling exhibition prepared by the Scriabin Museum and displayed across the Soviet Union. A collection of research studies and reminiscences about Scriabin was also published.

"What I appreciate most of all in Scriabin is that power of creative impetus, which great composers possess, and which expands the boundaries of the sphere assigned to art alone."

S. Feinberg[126]

Scriabin's music has become popular with music lovers everywhere. Among the Soviet musicologists lecturing on Scriabin is Professor Zukkerman, one of the most brilliant musicians and lecturers.

"In some works, such as the Fourth and Seventh Sonatas, *The Enigma, Vers la flamme*, and *Fragilité*, Stanislav Neuhaus almost achieves the 'disjunction' and 'nervousness' of playing characteristic of Scriabin himself."

A. Pasternak[127]

"His music does not merely excite, it astounds. It is all grandeur, all passion, eternally changeful flame."

M. Fedorov[128]

Tatiana Nikolayeva (b. 1924), a composer and pianist acclaimed for her performances of Scriabin's piano works.

Musicologist Arnold Alschwang (1898-1960).

Renowned pianist and pedagogue Heinrich Neuhaus.

Pianist Vladimir Sofronitzky (1901-1961), the best interpreter of
Scriabin's piano works.

Margarita Fedorov (b. 1927), a pianist whose repertoire includes all of Scriabin's works.

1962 saw the première of the ballet *Scriabiniana,* staged by Goleizovsky at the Bolshoi. The ballet score (an orchestration of Scriabin's piano works) was by Rogal-Levitzky.

When creating *Scriabiniana,* Goleizovsky's aim was not to illustrate music with dance, but to express through dance the music's inner essence.

Using Scriabin's rough sketches and notes (now in the Museum), Alexander Nemtin wrote *L'Acte préalable* for the 100th anniversary of the composer's birth. This work (very close to the symphonic poem *Prometheus* in both style and form) was first performed in Moscow on March 16, 1973.

The apartment where Scriabin spent the last three years of his life was turned into the Scriabin State Museum. Scriabin manuscripts are kept there, and extensive research on the composer's heritage is carried on. The Museum also holds regular concerts and recording nights. Visitors come to the Museum not only from all over the USSR but from other lands as well. The visitors' book is a graphic illustration of their impressions.

"Those who have always admired Scriabin's works, especially the ones of his later years, are deeply moved when they enter this house—the private environment, the spiritual world of the great composer."

Alejo Carpentier,
Cuban writer (1961)[129]

The Scriabin recitals given by Sofronitzky in the Museum are absolutely unforgettable. They were the highest peak of Sofronitzky's art.

"I will always cherish the sacred memory of the happiness of casting a single glance at the essence of the work of so great a composer as Scriabin was."

Van Cliburn (1960)[130]

"On the occasion of the Alexander Scriabin centennial, I present to the Scriabin Museum in Moscow the original manuscripts of his Fifth Sonata and the orchestral score of *the Poem of Ecstasy.* I do it in memory of my husband Alfred Laliberté, who was a student and friend of Scriabin from 1907 to 1911, and to whom the Master himself gave these manuscripts."

Madeleine Laliberté,
Moscow, August 11, 1971[131]

Scriabin was the first composer to introduce light—"Luce"—in a symphonic score, marking the color of the keys with different notes. Engineer A.E. Mozer constructed a color keyboard based on the technology of Scriabin's time.

Soviet engineer K.A. Leontiev was the first to give a scientific basis to the concept of color music; he created an experimental color music device based on modern technology.

In 1953, E.A. Murzin founded an experimental studio at the Scriabin Museum to work on color music and on the expansion of harmonic timbre capacities. He also designed the projects for

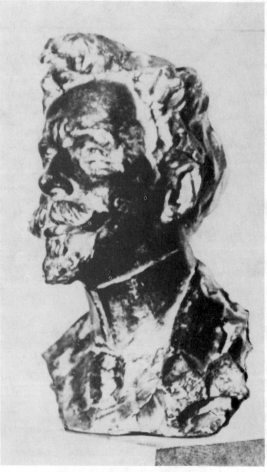

Scriabin. Sculpture by Sudbinin. Biarritz, 1908.

the light-and-color hall and the musical instrument named "ANS" (Scriabin's initials) which were built at the museum.

After Murzin's death, the experimental studio, now headed by Malkov, has continued to develop his ideas both in the realm of electronic music and color music.

The student design bureau "Prometheus" was founded at the Kazan Aircraft Institute to work on Scriabin's idea of color music.

The 1971-1972 concert season was devoted to the Scriabin centennial; concert series and individual concerts were held across the country, as well as conferences and lectures.

At the Scriabin centennial meeting, Rodion Shchedrin read the address of Dmitri Shostakovich, who could not attend because of illness.

"We are gathered today in this hall, sanctified by the great traditions of Russian music, to pay homage to the memory of an artist of genius, Alexander Scriabin. This outstanding composer rightly occupies an honorable place among the greats of world music.

"Scriabin's work is very close and dear to us, his compatriots, men and women of the first socialist country which opened up new horizons for humanity in the 20th century. We all remember that soon after the victory of the October Revolution, the Soviet Government adopted a plan for memorial monuments, a plan signed by Lenin. And among the names that were the pride and the glory of our national culture we find the name of Alexander Scriabin. The choice was not fortuitous—it underscored the message that Scriabin's heritage was needed by the builders of the new society, that it was living and would live for many generations.

"And this has proved to be true. Today, Scriabin's music can be heard in the concert halls of dozens of our cities, and also on radio and television. His symphonic works are in the repertoires of the leading orchestras and conductors; they have been recorded time and time again. The popularity of the composer's piano works is inexhaustible; pianists of all countries have turned to them. And, undoubtedly, new generations of listeners are entering and will enter the fascinating and unique world of Scriabin's music, and find themselves carried away by its inspired sweep, its elevated poetry.

"It is natural that Scriabin's works should be played especially often and very extensively in this season, when not only this country but the entire world, following the decision of the World Peace Council, is celebrating the centennial of one of the great masters of Russian art. There have been many studies, books and articles dealing with Scriabin's heritage; for several decades it was a subject of fervent debate and scholarly discussion. Today, the discussions are over, for the composer's enduring and important place in the history of 20th-century music has been tested by time itself.

"Scriabin lived and created his works in a turbulent era that saw so many events of tremendous social and political

A page of the manuscript of the *Prometheus* score.

131

Choreographer Kasian Goleizovsky (1892-1971), creator of *Scriabiniana*.

Famed composer Rodion Shchedrin (right) with his colleague Tikhon Khrennikov (left) and president of Paganiniana Publications Dr. Herbert R. Axelrod (center).

133

significance, such revolutionary changes in the life of the people. He was a son of that era. No matter how abstract or Utopian Scriabin's philosophical conceptions were, his music, like the work of every great artist, reflected many omens of the coming storm. It is not an exaggeration to say that his music was on the side of those who fought against tyranny for freedom and justice. There was ample reason why many of his contemporaries sensed in Scriabin's music a breath of the revolutionary storm, an acute presentiment, even a call for it. It was no accident that from the first post-revolutionary years his music did not lose its significance, but even became more in harmony with the spirit of the new listener, with the atmosphere of the new life.

"That is why it seems to me extremely appropriate to apply to Scriabin, to his contradictory and complicated character, the famous lines of his contemporary—Alexander Blok:

Forgive his gloom, his desolation,
For that is not his hidden might.
He is a child of good and light,
He is the joy of liberation!

"Scriabin is close to us today not only as a herald of the purifying revolutionary storm but also as a musical innovator who strove to open up new sources of musical expression, new ways of influencing the audience. And he succeeded in creating an exceptionally original musical language, a unique world of sound images.

"His contemporaries were shaken by the boldness of his harmonies, the whimsicality of his rhythms, the beauty of his melodies, imbued now with enchanting lyricism, now with vibrant strength. But today, after several decades, we clearly see that his innovation was deeply rooted in tradition, in the best sense of the word, in the achievements of the great classics of Russian and world music. That is why we realize now what a deep trace Scriabin's quests and discoveries have left, what an influence he had even on those composers whose development took a very different course. We are grateful to Scriabin for extending the boundaries of our art by his inexhaustible fantasy and his brilliant talent. We also cherish him for his faith in the transformative power of art, in its ability to ennoble the human soul, to bring harmony to people's lives. Of course, in the harsh conditions of the early years of this century, his faith remained an unattainable, although radiant, dream. It was the Great Revolution that not only brought freedom to the people but also liberated Art and enabled it to fulfill the glorious mission that was the dream and the passionate belief of the great Russian musician Alexander Scriabin."

Dmitri Shostakovich[132]

Dmitry Shostakovich (1906-1975).

"The history of Russian music is illuminated by great names. Today we celebrate the centennial of Alexander Scriabin, a great composer of our land. Every outstanding composer creates his own world of sound. Scriabin's world is unique and profoundly poetic. Fiery, dazzling exhilaration and crystal-clear lyricism, refined artistry and a passionate quest for happiness, light, joy and truth—this is what his music is about.

"Scriabin's music is piercingly sincere. It is rich in emotions, full of creative fervor and spiritual uplift. . .

"During the last years of his life, Scriabin dreamed of a synthetic art which would harmoniously unite music and dance, word and color, motion and the intoxicating fragrance of the flowers and grasses of the fields. We cannot accept the philosophy that accompanied Scriabin's dreams, but his belief in the elevating and emotive power of music is close and understandable to the present generations.

"And, of course, we also value Scriabin as a musical precursor of the great events that were to unfold soon after his untimely death. He was, as Lunacharsky said, one of petrels of the Revolution.

"In his work Scriabin turned again and again to the image of fire, of flame. I hope I am not mistaken in saying that the central image in Scriabin's music is Prometheus, who dared, as the beautiful ancient myth says, to steal fire from the gods and give it to people, to teach them trades and arts. We find this image appealing.

"And today we bow our heads to the memory of the great Russian poet of sound, whose music has given, gives, and will give to men and women, for years to come, happiness, inspiration, and pride in the power of the human creative spirit."

Rodion Shchedrin[133]

Program of a Scriabin recital by Margarita Fedorov.

Творчество А.Н. Скрябина близко
и дорого нам - его соотечественникам,
людям первой страны социализма,
открывшей человечеству новые
горизонты в двадцатом веке.

3 III 1972   Д Шостакович

"The work of Alexander Scriabin is close and dear to us, his compatriots, men and women of the first socialist country which opened up
new horizons for humanity in the twentieth century." Autograph by
Dmitry Shostakovich.

Notes to Text

List of literary sources
The list contains the following abbreviations;
GSCMMC - Glinka State Central Museum of Musical Culture
SSM - Scriabin State Museum

[1] N. Miaskovsky, "Tchaikovsky and Beethoven," *Collection of materials in 2 volumes,* 2nd ed. (Moscow: 1964), vol. 2, p. 68.

[2] B. Asafiev, *Russian music. The 19th and Beginning of the 20th Century,* (Leningrad: 1968), p. 180.

[3] N. Kashkin, "From reminiscences about Scriabin," *Musical Contemporary* (St. Petersburg, 1916), book 4/5, pp. 112-113.

[4] L. Scriabin, "Reminiscences," in the book: *Alexander Scriabin, 1915-1940: Collection for the 25th Anniversary of the Composer's Death* (Moscow - Leningrad: 1940), p. 7.

[5] Ibid., pp. 7-8.

[6] Ibid., p. 11.

[7] Ibid.

[8] L. Limantov, "Reminiscences," in the book: *Alexander Scriabin,* op. cit., p. 26.

[9] J. Engel, "Scriabin: A biographical essay," *Musical Contemporary,* op. cit., p. 21.

[10] L. Scriabin, "Reminiscences," op. cit., p. 13.

[11] A. Scriabin, The text for a youthful "Ballade." Autograph. SSM, No. 216.

[12] L. Scriabin, "Reminiscences," op. cit., p. 13.

[13] L. Limantov, "Reminiscences," op. cit., p. 28.

[14] J. Engel, "Scriabin . . .," op. cit., pp. 23-24.

[15] M. Presmann, "Reminiscences," *Alexander Scriabin,* op. cit., p. 33.

[16] Quoted from J. Engel, "Scriabin . . .," op. cit., p. 27.

[17] A. Ossovsky, "Young Scriabin," *Selected Articles and Reminiscences* (Leningrad: 1961), pp. 326-327.

[18] Ibid, pp. 323-324.

[19] L. Scriabin, "Reminiscences," op. cit., p. 14.

[20] A. Scriabin, *Letters,* compiled and edited by A. Kashperov (Moscow: 1965), pp. 49-50.

[21] A. Ossovsky, "Young Scriabin," op. cit., p. 327.

[22] Quoted from B. Schloezer, *A. Scriabin: A Monograph about the Person and his Work* (Berlin: "Grani" Publications, 1923), vol. 1, p. 90.

[23] Scriabin's notes. "Russian Propylaea," vol. 6 of *Materials on the History of Russian Thought and Literature* (Moscow: 1919), p. 121.

[24] L. Scriabin, "Reminiscences," op. cit., p. 17.

[25] A. Scriabin, *Letters*, op. cit., p. 56.

[26] Ibid, p. 84.

[27] Ibid, P. 85.

[28] Quoted from A. Scriabin, *Letters*, op. cit., p. 90.

[29] Quoted from L. Danilevich, *A. Scriabin* (Moscow: 1953), p. 17.

[30] A. Scriabin, *Letters*, op. cit., p. 103.

[31] Ibid., p. 107.

[32] Quoted from V. Delson, *Scriabin*, (Moscow: 1971), p. 68.

[33] Quoted from J. Engel, "Scriabin . . .," op. cit., p. 37.

[34] A. Scriabin, *Letters*, op. cit., p. 141.

[35] Ibid., p. 145.

[36] Ibid., p. 131.

[37] *Correspondence between Scriabin and Belaieff: 1894-1903* (Petrograd: 1922), p. 75.

[38] V. Bulgakov, *Tolstoy in the Last Year of His Life*, (Moscow: 1960), p. 285.

[39] N. Gusev and A. Goldenweiser, *Tolstoy and Music: Reminiscences* (Moscow: 1953), pp. 23-30.

[40] A. Scriabin, *Letters*, p. 107.

[41] J. Engel, "Scriabin . . .," op. cit., p. 39.

[42] Ibid., p. 40.

[43] Quoted from A. Scriabin, *Letters*, p. 179.

[44] Ibid., p. 183.

[45] Eu. Gunst, *Scriabin and His Work*, (Moscow: 1915), pp. 27-28.

[46] Quoted from V. Delson, *Scriabin*, p. 284.

[47] Nemenov-Lunz, "From reminiscences of a pupil." Typewritten. SSM, No. 8, pp. 5, 8, 9.

[48] A. Nezhdanova, Materials and Studies (Moscow: 1967), p. 58.

[49] A. Scriabin, *Letters*, p. 261.

[50] Ibid., p. 208.

[51] Ibid., p. 238.

[52] Ibid., p. 224.

[53] A. Ossovsky, *Foreword to Scriabin's Letters to Liadov*, ("Orpheus" Publications: 1922), book 1, p. 160.

[54] Quoted from A. Scriabin, *Letters*, p. 243.

[55] S. Trubetzkoy, "Publicist Articles," *Complete Works*, vol. 2, (Moscow: 1907), p. 386.

[56] Quoted from A. Scriabin, *Letters*, p. 278.

[57] L. Scriabin, "Reminiscences," p. 23.

[58] A. Gorky, "Song of the Stormy Petrel," *Selected works in 2 vol.* (Leningrad: 1963), vol. 1, p. 281.

[59] Scriabin's notes, "Russian Propylaea," vol. 6, p. 122.

[60] A. Alschwang, *Selected Works in 2 Volumes (Moscow: 1964), vol. 1, p. 168.*

[61] B. Pasternak, "About Scriabin and Chopin," *Soviet Music*, no. 1, 1967, p. 99.

[62] A. Scriabin, *Letters,* p. 293.

[63] Scriabin's Fourth Sonata in F sharp Major. Scriabin, text to the Fourth Sonata, *Music,* no. 3, 1910, p. 69.

[64] L. Sabaneyev, *Reminiscences of Scriabin,* (Moscow: 1925), p. 255.

[65] Quoted from A. Scriabin, *Letters,* p. 289.

[66] Ibid., p. 357.

[67] Ibid., p. 493.

[68] Ibid., p. 305.

[69] Ibid., pp. 339-340.

[70] A. Scriabin, *Letters,* p. 372.

[71] Ibid, p. 415.

[72] R. Plekhanov, "Reminiscences," in the book *Alexander Scriabin,* p. 65.

[73] G. Plekhanov, "Letters to Dr. Bogorodsky" in the book *Plekhanov as a Literary Critic* (Moscow: 1933), p. 167.

[74] Quoted from A. Alschwang, *Selected Works,* p. 176.

[75] T. Schloezer, Letter to Nemenov-Lunz of February, 20, 1906, Autograph, SSM, no. 496, p. 11.

[76] A. Scriabin, *Letters,* p. 454.

[77] T. Schloezer, Letter to Nemenov-Lunz of April 4, 1907, Autograph, SSM, no. 504.

[78] Scriabin's notes, "Russian Propylaea," vol. 6, p. 139.

[79] A. Scriabin, *Letters,* p. 343.

[80] Ibid., p. 475.

[81] M. Nemenov-Lunz, "From reminiscences of a pupil," op. cit., pp. 13 and 18.

[82] Ibid.

[83] T. Schloezer, Letter to Nemenov-Lunz of May 23, 1907, Autograph, SSM, no. 507.

[84] A. Scriabin, *Letters,* p. 483.

[85] V. Valter, Review of the concert of January 31, 1909, in *Rech,* Feb. 2, 1909.

[86] M. Morozov, "From reminiscences," *Soviet Music,* no. 1, 1972, p. 128.

[87] *Marx and Engels on Art,* collection in 2 vol. (Moscow, 1976), vol. 1, p. 273.

[88] Quoted from A. Alschwang, Selected works in 2 volumes, vol. 1, p. 192.

[89] A. Alschwang, *A. Scriabin* (Moscow - Leningrad, 1945), p. 44.

[90] T. Schloezer, Letter to nemenov-Lunz of October 21, 1909, Autograph, SSM, no. 551.

[91] E. Bosquet, "Reminiscences of Scriabin," Typewritten, SSM, No. 120.

[92] Quoted from *Alexander Scriabin,* op. cit., pp. 233-234.

[93] A. Scriabin, *Letters,* p. 578.

[94] A. Pasternak, "Summer of 1903," *Noviy Mir (New World),* 1972, no. 1, pp. 209-210.

[95] Quoted from Ya. Milstein, *Konstantin Igumnov* (Moscow: 1975), p. 86.

[96] T. Schloezer, Letter to M. Schloezer of April, 26, 1910, Autograph, SSM, no. 560.

[97] T. Schloezer, Letter to M. Schloezer of May 3, 1910,

Autograph, SSM, no. 561.

[98] A. Scriabin, *Letters,* p. 610.

[99] Review of the concert in Vilno on November 14, 1913, the newspaper *Nasha Kopeika,* SSM, no. 2034, 2060.

[100] B. Schloezer's note on *L'Acte préalable,* "Russian Propylea," vol. 6, p. 100.

[101] From letters to Scriabin, in the book *Alexander Scriabin,* p. 234.

[102] L. Sabaneyev, *Reminiscences of Scriabin,* p. 167.

[103] A. Scriabin, *Letters,* p. 629.

[104] L. Sabaneyev, *Reminiscences of Scriabin,* p. 190.

[105] *Utro Rossii,* Jan. 20, 1913, SSM, no. 2177.

[106] A. Ossovsky, "Sergei Rachmaninoff," in the book *Reminiscences of Rachmaninoff,* compiled and edited by Z. Apetyan (Moscow: 1974), 4th edition, vol. 1, p. 370.

[107] A. Alschwang, "Julian Scriabin" in the book *Alexander Scriabin,* p. 242.

[108] K. Balmont, *Light-sound in Nature and Scriabin's Light Symphony* (Moscow: 1917), pp. 22-23.

[109] *Birzheviey vedomosti,* April 15, 1915.

[110] Ibid.

[111] B. Pasternak, "About Scriabin and Chopin," *Soviet Music,* no. 1, 1967, p. 101.

[112] Quoted from M. Lentulov, *Painter Aristarkh Lentulov: Reminiscences,* (Moscow: 1969), p. 95.

[113] Ibid., p. 95.

[114] Ibid., pp. 95-96.

[115] A. Lunacharsky, "Taneyev and Scriabin," in the book *In the Realm of Music* (Moscow: 1971), p. 143.

[116] B. Asafiev, *Russian music: the 19th and Beginning of the 20th Century,* p. 180.

[117] N. Miaskovsky, "St. Petersburg Letters," *Collection of Materials in 2 Volumes,* vol. 2, p. 102.

[118] S. Prokofiev, *Materials, Documents, and Reminiscences,* (Moscow: 1961), p. 638.

[119] D. Shostakovich, Opening speech at the gala evening in the Grand Hall of the Moscow Conservatory on January 6, 1972. Typewritten. GSCMMC.

[120] A. Alschwang, "Scriabin's philosophical system," *Selected Works in 2 Volumes,* vol. 1, p. 264.

[121] From the GSCMMC archives.

[122] From the SSM archives.

[123] From the SSM archives.

[124] A. Lunacharsky, "Taneyev and Scriabin," op. cit., p. 134.

[125] From the SSM archives.

[126] From the SSM archives.

[127] A. Pasternak, "Summer of 1903," op. cit., p. 210.

[128] From the SSM archives.

[129] Visitors book. SSM.

[130] Entry in the visitors book.

[131] M-me Laliberté's letter. SSM.

[132] From the GSCMMC archives.

[133] From the GSCMMC archives.

Index

(Page numbers in *italics* refer to illustrations.)

A

Aeschylus, 99
Akimenko, Fedor, 15, 114
Alexandrov, Anatoly, 34, *37*, 124
Alschwang, Arnold, 35, 77, 88, 99, 115, 124, *126*
Altschuler, Modest, 15, 88, 89, *92*, *100*, *102*, 103
Arensky, Anton, 9, 54
Asafiev, Boris, 34, 35, *122*, 124
Avierino, Nikolai, 55, *57*
Axelrod, Dr. Herbert R., *133*

B

Bach, Johann Sebastian, 14, 48
Balakirev, Mily, 59
Balmont, Konstantin, 15, 115
Baltrushaitis, Yu., *15*, 15, 108, 114
Beethoven, Ludwig van, 14, 20, 30, 34, 54, 99
Belaieff, Mitrofan, 14, 61, 62, 63, *65*, 66 (letter from), 68, 72, 73
Blok, Alexander, 21, 24, 115, 134
Blumenfeld, Felix, 15, 62, 83, *93*, 94, 95
Borovsky, Alexander, 114
Bosquet, Émile, 102
Brianchaninov, Alexander, 109
Bulgakov, V., 68
Busoni, Feruccio, 108
Buyukli, Vsevolod, 15, *18*, 55

C

Carpentier, Alejo, 130
Chaliapin, Fedor, 114
Chessin, Alexander, *96*
Chopin, Frédéric, *12*, 14, 20, 25, 26, 31, 54, 63
Cliburn, Van, 130
Conus, Georgi, 48
Cooper, Emil, 15, *16*, 95
Cui, César, 31, 69

D

Debussy, Claude, 14
Dobrowen, Isai, 15
Doret, Gustave, 63
Dostoyevsky, Fedor, 115
Duncan, Isadora, 109, *113*

E

Engel, Julius, 14, 34, 49, 69, 76

F

Fedorov, Margarita, 125, *129*, 135
Feinberg, Samuel, 34, 35, 124, 125
Fried, Oscar, 15

G

George, Eugène, 63
Glazunov, Alexander, 14, 34, 62, *67*, 77, *78*, 82, 115
Glière, Reinhold, 114, 115
Gnessin, Mikhail, 34, 124
Goldenweiser, Alexander, 14, 15, 68, *69*, 114, 125
Goleizovsky, Kasian, 130, *132*
Golovanov, Nikolai, 35
Gorky, Maxim (Alexei Peshkov), 20, 24, 77
Gunst, Evgeni, 15, 34, 69

H

Hoffmann, Joseph, 15, 68

I

Igumnov, Konstantin, 15, *19*, 103, 114
Ivanov, Vyacheslav, 15, 114

J

Jurgenson, Pyotr, 59, 102

K

Kachalov, Vasily, 109

Karatygin, Vyacheslav, 34
Karlowicz, Mechislav, 34
Kashkin, N., 24, 43
Keneman, Fedor, 9, *11*
Khrennikov, Tikhon, *133*
Koonen, Alissa, 109
Koussevitzky, Sergei, 15, 49, 94, *97*, 102, 103, 108, 114
Krein, Alexander, 15, 124

L

Laliberté, Alfred, 130
Laliberté, Madeleine, 130
Lamoureux, Charles, 68
Lenin, Vladimir, 34, 119, 131
Lentulov, Aristarch, *119*, 119
Lentulov, Mrs. M., 119
Leontiev, K.A., 130
Levin, Iosif, 9, 55, 59, 68
Liadov, Konstantin, 14, 25, 34, 62, *67*, 73, 75
Limantov, L., 48, 49, *52*
Liszt, Franz, 14, 26, 27, *28*, 30, 59, 69, 99
Lunacharsky, Anatoly, 30, 34, 119, 125

M

Maksimov, Leonid, 9
Malko, Nikolai, *25*, 35
Marx, Karl, 99
Medtner, Nikolai, 24, 31
Mendelssohn, Felix, 48
Mengelberg, Willem, 14, 15, 108
Meychik, Mark, *32*
Meyerhold, Vsevolod, 25
Miaskovsky, Nikolai, 20, 34, 114, *123*, 124
Mogilevsky, Alexander, 15
Monighetti, Olga, 49, *53*
Monighetti, Zinaida, 82
Morozov, Magarita, 89, 94, *94*, 95

Mozart, Wolfgang Amadeus, 59
Mozer, A.E. 130
Mravinsky, Evgeni, 35
Murzin, E.A., 130, 131
Mussorgsky, Modest, 14
Myers, Charles, 109

N

Nebolsin, Vasily, 35
Nemenov-Lunz, Maria, 15, 72, 88, 89, *91*, 99
Nemirovich-Danchenko, Vladimir, 119
Nemtin, Alexander, 130
Neuhaus, Heinrich, 35, 125, *127*
Neuhaus, Stanislav, 125
Newmarch, Rosa, 102, 109
Nezhdanov, Antonina, 72, *76*
Nikisch, Arthur, 15, *17*, 77, 83
Nikolaiev, Leonid, 114
Nikolayeva, Tatiana, *125*

O

Ossovsky, Alexander, 54, 55, 59, 73, 114

P

Pasternak, Boris, 25, 77, 115
Pasternak, Leonid, 15, 99 (painting by), 103, *105*
Plekhanov, Georgy, 21, 88, 119
Plekhanov, Mrs. R., 88
Pressman, Matvei, 54
Prokofiev, Sergei, 31, 34, 124

R

Rachmaninoff, Sergei, 9, *10*, 14, 15, 20, 24, 31, 39, 94, 114
Rimsky-Korsakov, Nikolai, 14, 15, 25, 26, 31, 34, 62, *67*, *71*, 72, 73, 77
Rodin, Auguste, 94
Rogal-Levitzky, Dmitry, 130
Romanovsky, Gavriil, 114
Rosenov, Emil, 55, 64
Rubinstein, Anton, 48

S

Sabaneyev, Leonid, 15, 34, *108*, 109
Safonov, Vassily, 9, 20, 49, 54, *56*, 62, 69, 73, 76, 79, 88, *92*

Saminsky, Lazar, 34
Saradiev, Konstantin, 15
Sargent, John, 102
Schloezer, Boris, 24, 82, 108
Schloezer, Tatiana, 24, 69, 83, *87*, 88, 89, 94, 99, 103, 108, *108*, 109, *111*
Schlözer, Pavel, 69
Schumann, Robert, 31
Scriabin, Alexander (illustrations), *8*, *15*, *40-41*, *46*, *47*, *50*, *58*, *64*, *74*, *81*, *90*, *98*, *99*, *101*, *103*, *107*, *108*, *109*, *111*, *117*
Scriabin, Alexander (works by):
L'Acte préalable, 15, 31, 34, 108, 130
Allegro Op. 4, 68
Ballade, 48, 49
Concerto for Piano and Orchestra, 69, 88
Désir, 30, 109
Dreams, 72, 73, 77, 124
Enigma, 109, 125
Etrangeté, 31
Etude in C-sharp minor, 54, 68, 82, 84
Fragilité, 125
Impromptus Op. 7, 68
Impromptu Op. 12, No. 1 (F-sharp major), 63
Impromptu Op. 14, No. 2 (F-sharp minor), 63
Masque, 31
Mazurkas Op. 3, 68
Mystery, The, 15, 108, 109
Nocturne in A-flat major, *9*, 48
Nocturne in F-sharp minor, 54
Poème ailé, 31
Poème satanique, 31
Poem of Ecstasy, The, 24, 35, 36, 38, 89, 94, 95, 96, 124, 125, 130
Prelude Op. 11, No. 5, 109
Prelude Op. 11, No. 12 (G-sharp minor), 63
Prelude Op. 11, No. 17 (A-flat major), 63
Prelude Op. 11, No. 18 (F minor), 63
Prelude Op. 11, No. 23 (F major), 63
Prelude Op. 16 (B major), 26,

54
Prelude Op. 16, No. 2 (G-sharp minor), 63
Prelude Op. 39, No. 12 (G-sharp minor), 109
Prelude and Nocturne Op. 9, 68
Prometheus ("The Poem of Fire"), 29, 30, 31, 68, 69, 99, 102, 109, 119, 130, *131*
Sonata No. 1 for Piano, 31, 63
Sonata No. 2 for Piano, 48, 68, 69, 72
Sonata No. 3 for Piano, 69
Sonata No. 4 for Piano, 24, 31, 35, 48, 82, 125
Sonata No. 5 for Piano, 31, 34, 35, 130
Sonata No. 7 for Piano, 25, 108, 125
Sonata No. 8, 108
Sonata No. 9 for Piano, 25, 26, 27, 31, 48, 109
Symphony No. 1, 73, 75, 76, 79, 108
Symphony No. 2, 76
Symphony No. 3 ("The Divine Poem"), 26, 30, 35, 77, 82, 83, 88, 89, 95, 124
Vers la flamme, 31, 125
Scriabin, Ariadna, 114
Scriabin, Helena, 114
Scriabin, Julian, *111*, 114, 115, *116*
Scriabin, Lev, 114
Scriabin, Lubov (the composer's aunt), *40-41*, 43, 48, 49, 59, 76
Scriabin (née Shchetinin), Lubov, the composer's mother, 43, *44*
Scriabin, Maria, 114
Scriabin, Marina, 114
Scriabin, Nikolai (the composer's father), *40-41*, 43, *45*, *47*
Scriabin, Rimma, 114
Scriabin (née Isakovich), Vera, 15, 42, 69, *70*, 73, 77, 82, 83, *86*
Sekerin, Natalia, 59, *60*, 62, 63, 68
Shaw, George Bernard, 102
Shchedrin, Rodion, *120-121*, 131,

133, 135
Shostakovich, Dmitry, 124, 131, 134, *134,* 136 (autograph)
Sigogne, Emile, 99
Sofronitzky, Vladimir, 35, 125, *128,* 130
Stanislavsky, Konstantin, 109, *112,* 119
Stasov, Vassily, 31, 62, 83
Sterl, Robert, 108
Strauss, Richard, 14
Stravinsky, Igor, 25, 108, *110*
Sudbinin, S., 94, 130 (sculpture by)

Szymanowski, Karol, 34

T
Tabakov, Mikhail, *36*
Tairov, Alexander, 25, 109
Taneyev, Sergei, 9, 25, 26, 30, 34, 48, 49, *51,* 55, 99
Tchaikovsky, Peter, 14, 20, 25, 26, 30, 34, 43
Tolstoy, Leo, 68, 69
Tree, Sir Beerbohm, 109
Trubetzkoy, Sergei, 14, 76, *80*

V
Valter, V., 94

Vrubel, Mikhail, 24

W
Wagner, Richard, *13,* 14, 26, 27
Wood, Sir Henry, 15, 29, 102

Y
Yavorsky, Boris, 114

Z
Zhilayev, Nikolai, 15
Ziloti, Alexander, 15, 102, *104,* 114
Zverev, Nikolai, 9, 48, 49